The Music
Library

The History
of Indie Rock

Other books in this series include:

The Music Library

The History of Indie Rock

By Jennifer Skancke

LUCENT BOOKS
An imprint of Thomson Gale, a part of The Thomson Corporation

Detroit • New York • San Francisco • New Haven, Conn. • Waterville, Maine • London

For Ceci and T-Bone

For more information, contact
Lucent Books
27500 Drake Rd.
Farmington Hills, MI 48331-3535
Or you can visit our Internet site at http://www.gale.com

LIBRARY OF CONGRESS CATALOGING-IN-PUBLICATION DATA

Skancke, Jennifer.
The history of indie rock / by Jennifer Skancke.
    p. cm. — (The music library)
Includes bibliographical references and index.
ISBN 13: 978-1-59018-736-4
ISBN 10: 1-59018-736-9 (hardcover : alk. paper)
1. Alternative rock music—History and criticism—Juvenile literature. I. Title.
ML3534.S567 2007
781.66--dc22
                                                          2006022547

Printed in the United States of America

• Contents •

• Foreword •

In the nineteenth century, English novelist Charles Kingsley wrote, "Music speaks straight to our hearts and spirits, to the very core and root of our souls. . . . Music soothes us, stirs us up . . . melts us to tears." As Kingsley stated, music is much more than just a pleasant arrangement of sounds. It is the resonance of emotion, a joyful noise, a human endeavor that can soothe the spirit or excite the soul. Musicians can also imitate the expressive palette of the earth, from the violent fury of a hurricane to the gentle flow of a babbling brook.

The word *music* is derived from the fabled Greek muses, the children of Apollo who ruled the realms of inspiration and imagination. Composers have long called upon the muses for help and insight. Music is not merely the result of emotions and pleasurable sensations, however.

Music is a discipline subject to formal study and analysis. It involves the juxtaposition of creative elements such as rhythm, melody, and harmony with intellectual aspects of composition, theory, and instrumentation. Like painters

mixing red, blue, and yellow into thousands of colors, musicians blend these various elements to create classical symphonies, jazz improvisations, country ballads, and rock-and-roll tunes.

Throughout centuries of musical history, individual musical elements have been blended and modified in infinite ways. The resulting sounds may convey a whole range of moods, emotions, reactions, and messages. Music, then, is both an expression and reflection of human experience and emotion.

The foundations of modern musical styles were laid down by the first ancient musicians who used wood, rocks, animal skins—and their own bodies—to re-create the sounds of the natural world in which they lived. With their hands, their feet, and their very breath they ignited the passions of listeners and moved them to their feet. The dancing, in turn, had a mesmerizing and hypnotic effect that allowed people to transcend their worldly concerns. Through music they could achieve a level of shared experience that could not be found in other forms of communication. For this reason, music has always been part of religious endeavors, from ancient Egyptian religious ceremonies to modern Christian masses. And it has inspired dance movements from kings and queens spinning the minuet to punk rockers slamming together in a mosh pit.

By examining musical genres ranging from Western classical music to rock and roll, readers will find a new understanding of old music and develop an appreciation for new sounds. Books in Lucent's Music Library focus on the music, the musicians, the instruments, and on music's place in cultural history. The songs and artists examined may be easily found in the CD and sheet music collections of local libraries so that readers may study and enjoy the music covered in the books. Informative sidebars, annotated bibliographies, and complete indexes highlight the text in each volume and provide young readers with many opportunities for further discussion and research.

What Is Indie Rock?

In 2001 not many people had heard of Death Cab for Cutie, an indie (or independent) rock band from Seattle, Washington. By 2006, however, any fan of popular music was likely to say that Death Cab for Cutie was one of the most popular bands in the indie rock scene. The band showed up on numerous top-ten lists of indie rock groups. Its music was played frequently on commercial radio stations and was even featured on the popular television shows *The O.C.* and *Six Feet Under* and in the 2005 movie *Wedding Crashers.* In just a few years Death Cab for Cutie rose from relative obscurity to become one of the most recognizable bands in America.

Death Cab for Cutie formed in 1997. The group released its first four albums on Seattle's independent record label, Barsuk Records. Known for its dreamy pop sound, created by melding electronic music with vocals and guitars, Death Cab for Cutie ap-pealed to a large underground audience as well as to critics of independent music.

With the release of its fourth album, *Transatlanticism*, in 2003, the band sold 225,000 copies in the first year. Suddenly the relatively unknown band was receiving attention from the media and major record labels, which wanted to capitalize on the band's underground popularity. One year later the band signed with Atlantic Records, a major label in the music industry, and it officially broke into the mainstream music world. In 2005 its song "Soul Meets Body" from its *Plans* album reached number five on the U.S. Modern Rock Chart and number sixty on the U.S. Hot 100. The band also received a 2005 Grammy Award for the album. Death Cab for Cutie represents just one of many indie rock bands that exemplify the growing popularity of the independent music scene.

Critics and music fans vary in their opinions about whether bands like

Death Cab for Cutie are still technically indie rock since they are no longer signed to an independent label. Until recently, being on an independent label had been the defining characteristic of the indie rock genre. *Indie rock* was a term created in the late 1990s by major record companies, publicists, and radio formatters to describe those bands and artists making rock music on independent labels outside of the mainstream. Now that indie rock has entered into the mainstream, many critics wonder what will happen to the independent scene that gained its identity as the alternative to the pop and rock music industry.

No Identifiable Sound

Indie rock is difficult to define not only because of crossover appeal but also because the music has never had a specific sound, unlike other musical genres such as jazz, blues, or country. There are no telltale sounds like country music's guitar twang or signature motifs such as jazz's improvisations. Although indie rock is a form of rock and roll and uses guitars, basses, and drums in the basic band unit, the music encompasses a wide range of sounds. For instance, the

White Stripes, a minimalist rock duo from Detroit, plays simple compositions with a guitar, piano, and drums. The Decemberists from Portland, Oregon, however, is a five-piece band that uses instruments like the accordion and upright bass. Though quite different in their sounds and approaches,

Lead singer Ben Gibbard performs with indie rockers Death Cab for Cutie. Death Cab produced its first four albums with an independent record label in Seattle, Washington.

Some indie bands like the Decemberists incorporate nontraditional rock instruments into their music.

both bands are considered part of the indie rock genre.

What makes the White Stripes and the Decemberists indie rock then? Most frequently indie rock refers to rock music made by bands that are signed to an independent record label. Indie labels are considered to be any label other than one of the "Big Four" record companies—Universal Music Group, Sony BMG Music Entertainment, Warner Music Group, and EMI Group—or their affiliates, which are smaller labels owned by the Big Four. As of 2005, these four record companies held close to 80 percent of the U.S. music market and about 70 percent of the world music market. These labels also own their own distribution channels, giving them a lot of control over the recording and marketing of music.

Independent labels have provided an alternative for those artists who find it difficult to get a recording contract with one of the major labels. Independent record labels are smaller than the major labels and usually take chances on new groups as well as bands that make music that does not fit the pop market. There is a lot more room for experimentation on indie labels, whereas artists signed to one of the major labels are often tightly controlled by the company. As such, indie artists are able to maintain some degree of creative control over the sound and distribution of their music.

An Illusory Ideal

The expansion of indie record labels in the 1990s, and ultimately indie rock, had a lot to do with the dissatisfaction many musicians and artists felt with the major record labels. Some artists were concerned that the labels had all the power when it came to making and selling music. Others were put off by the fact that major labels often were not interested in music that they did not think would immediately capture the attention of the buying public. Many artists and bands preferred to make music that was different from music receiving mass airplay and often experimented with new sounds and instrumentation. These artists were soon dubbed *independent*.

As such, indie rock has often been thought of by those in the independent music scene as being "purer" and "less corporatized" than mainstream pop music. Perhaps due to the rise of the independent label scene in the late 1970s and early 1980s as an alternative to the corporate rock scene—in which bands were often created by the studios or else had their sounds adulterated and streamlined to meet marketability—indie rock has been touted as being more creative and artistic because it is supposedly less manufactured than some of the music put out by major labels. Indie rock has gained a reputation for being the ideal way of making music because indie rock artists tend to experiment, write their own music and lyrics, and avoid overproduction. Scholar Ryan Hibbett describes indie rock's appeal as outsider music:

Because indie rock gains its appeal through its defiance of mainstream conventions, because it does not meet the protocols for radio or music television . . . it cannot achieve a mass following. Thus indie enthusiasts turn to symbolic value, defending what they like as "too good" for radio, too innovative and challenging to interest those blasting down the highway. They become the scholars and conservators of "good" music.[1]

Indie rock fans tend to believe that their favorite musicians are less concerned with being rock stars and are more interested in making music without compromise. Many artists, in fact, claim that they choose to remain independent rather than become part of the mainstream so that their artistic vision will not be warped by corporate pressures. As a result, this ideal of purity is attributed to indie rock.

Although plenty of bands adhere to this independent ethic, many indie rock artists use independent labels as stepping stones to signing with major labels. Sometimes bands start out on an indie label and then build a large enough fan base to attract a major label. However, once the group's music is available to the public, most bands ultimately seek the recognition and money offered by a major label deal. Some indie music purists consider those indie rock musicians who have signed with a major label sellouts—meaning they have forgone their independent ideals in order to achieve fame and make a lot of money.

The purist ideal further complicates the term *indie rock* and blurs the boundary between maintaining artistic idealism and taking advantage of an opportunity for mainstream success. This issue raises several difficult questions: Is a band that starts out on an independent label still technically an indie if it signs with a major label? What if the band retains its independent ethic and sense of experimentation; would or should it still be considered an indie rock band?

The Next Cycle of Rock

While some argue about whether being signed to an independent label or having an independent spirit qualifies a band as indie rock, others see indie rock as nothing but a marketing ploy to sell music. Music, particularly rock music, tends to evolve in cycles. Eventually what is popular in the mainstream becomes tired and old, and record companies look to tap into the newest underground rock music being played by teenagers in small local scenes. Once the industry latches on to a successful underground music, they need a term to categorize it so that it has a place in music stores and on commercial radio.

Indie rock is the latest music in this cycle of renewal. In the 1960s psychedelic music brought a counterculture to mainstream awareness, as did punk in the 1970s, hardcore and college rock in the 1980s, and grunge in the early 1990s. Indie rock evolved to become what it is (or is not) as a result

Jack White of the White Stripes wails through a guitar solo in San Diego, California. The indie rock genre encompasses a wide variety of musical styles and sounds.

of significant developments in the music industry during these earlier periods of music. For instance, indie rock is a youth-driven music much like punk was in the middle to late 1970s. It draws on the do-it-yourself ethic defined by the British underground punk scene and the American hardcore scene in the late 1970s and early 1980s. Like college rock did in the 1980s, indie rock taps into the youth market through college radio stations and networks of educated youth. And much like the grunge movement in the early 1990s, indie rock faces commercialization now that the term has been co-opted by the recording industry in order to sell music.

The historical connections illustrate that indie rock has strong roots, but as with grunge, the flowering of indie rock might signal its eventual demise. More optimistic observers contend, however, that it is just one more cycle in the ever-changing rock music scene. When the current indie rock is picked up by the mainstream, like psychedelia was in the 1960s and grunge was in the 1990s, it will drive other musicians underground, and a new music scene will emerge. The cycle—and the debates—will begin again.

Chapter One

Punk: The Angry Scream of Disaffected Youth

In November 1976 the Sex Pistols, an unheard-of punk rock band from London, England, released its first record single, "Anarchy in the UK." The song, which would eventually reach number thirty-eight on the U.K. singles chart, was an angry rant at the failures of the British government. It encouraged people to defy the government and live in a state of absolute freedom. Lead singer Johnny Rotten screamed the lyrics while proclaiming to be the Antichrist. Many people in England were terrified by the band's message. Its public behavior, including swearing on live television, and the near riots that followed its performances also contributed to the band's notoriety. Never before had a band expressed its anger so blatantly. The media immediately took notice, and the Sex Pistols were featured on the front pages of newspapers and magazines with headlines like "The Filth and the Fury." Almost overnight, punk rock music, which had until then existed in small underground music circles, entered the consciousness of mainstream audiences.

Though there were punk bands before the Sex Pistols, it popularized punk rock music and helped turn it into a popular music genre. Countless punk rock bands were formed in the wake of the Sex Pistols furor. Punk rock became an anthem for the disillusioned young people who identified with the anger and energy of the music. It allowed young people an outlet to express their dissatisfaction with society and the expectations placed on them. Punk rock also encouraged individuality, a quality that many young people felt had been lacking in mainstream rock and roll. Lyrics questioned the state of society and told listeners that things did not have to be as they seemed. Music critic Greil Marcus defines punk as treason "against the future society had planned for you; against your own impulse to say yes, to buy whatever others had put on the market. . . . Punk was a new music, a new social critique, but most of all it was a new kind of free speech."[2]

Although the first wave of punk rock lasted only a few short years, it laid the foundation for the indie rock scene that would emerge almost thirty years later. Like indie rock, punk was initially an outsider music that spoke to the youth. It was music that young people identified with and could call their own. Punk made being independent and speaking for oneself essential qualities in all youth music scenes that followed. In fact, this ideal would become the cornerstone to the development of the independent music scene.

The State of Rock and Roll

The term *punk rock* was developed in 1976 to describe the loud, fast, and angry music that was emerging as an alternative to mainstream rock-and-roll music. By the early 1970s rock and roll had existed for close to two decades and had developed into a major commodity. Popular rock bands like the Who, the Rolling Stones, and the Beatles were heavily promoted by their record labels. These bands dominated radio airwaves and embarked on major tours, selling out stadium-sized venues to adoring fans. Record labels clamored to sign similar acts in the hope of making a lot of money.

The popular rock bands at the time were tightly controlled by their record companies. The music was produced in elaborate recording studios using the latest studio technology to enhance the sound of a band's vocals and its instruments. Like all industries, the music industry tried to copy successful formulas. Record executives were mainly interested in bands that would appeal to mainstream audiences, so many major-label groups had songs with similar-sounding guitar riffs and familiar chord patterns. In addition, most songs had to be at least three minutes long to be played on commercial radio. There was little room for bands who were interested in experimentation.

While the record labels catered to—and helped shape—popular tastes, many young listeners grew tired of hearing the same select, radio-friendly songs over and over. Young musicians were also disenchanted with an industry-controlled music scene in which success was measured by expensive studio production and arena touring. They began to explore alternatives to satisfy their musical cravings. Some bands retreated to the "underground"—a term referring to a loose affiliation of artists who could not or did not want to break into the mainstream. In the underground, people could play any kind of music they wanted, and however they wanted to play it. The underground allowed plenty of room for experimentation.

Music from the Underground

As more musicians began to play an alternative style of rock and roll, many

Popular rock-and-roll bands like the Beatles dominated radio play and created elaborate albums thanks largely to major record labels.

small underground scenes formed throughout Britain and America. Small clubs and venues that catered to more experimental music sprang up in cities like London, New York, Los Angeles, and San Francisco. One underground music scene that would be influential to the burgeoning punk rock movement was the East Coast art and music scene that originated in New York in the mid-1960s.

The Velvet Underground was one of the most well-known and influential of the East Coast underground bands.

The band was put together by pop culture artist Andy Warhol in 1965 and would become known for its experimental sound and avant-garde influences. The band featured an electric viola, which was used to hold the same note, tone, or sound for lengthy periods of time and with little variation. Lead singer Lou Reed's lyrics were dark, confrontational, and grim, and they included subject matter that was not typically found in mainstream rock, such as sadomasochism, transvestitism, and heroin addiction. He wrote graphic lyrics at a time when drug abuse and sexual identity were taboo subjects in popular culture. His songs contained darker images as opposed to the clean love ballads from teen pop idols.

The music and lyrics of the Velvet Underground did not capture the attention of record labels or commercial radio. The band was able to gain a small and dedicated cult following as a result of some of its shows, which were accompanied by Warhol's pop art imagery and included his unusual set of friends. Scholar Ryan Hibbett refers to these performances as "lo-fi yet highly experimental," making the Velvet Underground "an edgier and poorly received alternative to the Beatles."[3] The audiences for these events were typically comprised of like-minded youth who were excited by the cultish atmosphere and the newness of the sounds.

Many listeners were inspired to start their own bands after hearing the Velvet Underground. Iggy Pop, lead singer of the Stooges, was moved to make music after hearing the band's record *The Velvet Underground & Nico.* Pop remembers becoming aware that it was possible to create music despite not having any prior musical knowledge or training. He recalls,

The Velvet Underground played music that defied the mainstream radio and record labels of the era.

"That record became very key for me, not just for what it said, and for how great it was, but also because I heard other people who could make good music—without being any good at music. It gave me hope."[4]

The Rise of Punk

Inspired by the Velvet Underground and other underground musicians, many young people formed their own bands and began playing small clubs, especially in New York City. Clubs like CBGBs and Max's Kansas City allowed unsigned bands to play original music. It was in these small clubs in the early- to mid-1970s that youth-oriented audiences discovered a new sound that was speaking to them. As the scene gained momentum, this new style of music came to be known as punk rock.

Many of the early clubs featured the first punk acts, including Television, the New York Dolls, Patti Smith, and the Ramones. These bands were not concerned with conformity and making music like popular rock bands. They were formed mainly of young people who had all been influenced by the counterculture of the 1960s and by the New York City art scene. They distrusted authority and embraced the rebel outsider image to establish their identities. They rejected popular music like disco and the progressive rock groups that prized instrumentation and clean vocals. Many could not identify with what they saw as the artifice of overproduced studio sounds. They wanted their rock and roll to be raw like the garage bands that blossomed in the middle to late 1960s.

Many of the musicians who played these clubs had no previous musical training. Their shows depended on energy, visual interest, volume, and audience participation in intimate spaces. They often played hard, fast, and out of tune. For instance, the New York Dolls were considered by most to be inept musicians. They used heavy drumming, minimal rhythm guitar, and a lead guitar that played unpredictable melodies. Lead singer David Johansen recalls, "People who saw the Dolls said, 'Hell, anybody can do this.' . . . I think what the Dolls did as far as being an influence on punk was that we showed that anybody could do it."[5]

The Ramones was also a punk band that did not have a background in music. However, its use of distorted guitars and fast tempos to create a simplistic but aggressive sound would come to characterize the abrasive side of punk music. The band emphasized the rhythm guitar and highlighted short guitar solos. Repeated bass lines and loud, thundering drums contributed to the aggressive feel of the songs. It used offbeat humor in its lyrics and in song titles such as "Suzy Is a Headbanger" and "Pinhead." Like most punk bands at the time, the Ramones was overlooked by the mainstream music industry, but the band built up a dedicated underground following.

The Safety-Pin Ethic

Not only did punk come to have a distinct sound, but it also became associated with a particular look. Many of these early punk bands created an image that appealed to young audiences. The look helped forge an identity for those punk musicians as well as fans. Band members often used their clothing to distinguish themselves from the way artists in the mainstream dressed. The New York Dolls wore makeup and dressed like women. The Ramones wore tight jeans, Chuck Taylor high-top tennis shoes, and black leather jackets. Yet Richard Hell, a member of the Neon Boys and Television before forming the Heartbreakers and the Voidoids, would have the strongest impact on the punk look.

Hell created what some critics came to call the safety-pin ethic. Hell styled his hair into tall spikes and wore torn clothes that he fastened together with safety pins. Hell believed that fashion should be cheap and accessible rather than flashy and expensive, like most of the outfits worn by disco fans and rock musicians. The tattered-and-torn look would become a punk staple later in the decade, especially after British entrepreneur Malcom McLaren

Early punk rockers the New York Dolls rejected the crisp, overproduced studio sound in favor of gritty, unpredictable guitars and heavy drumming.

The Punk Sound

The punk sound was raw and angry. Most rock music at the time had a polished sound that was created by high-tech studio equipment and expensive instruments. Artifice had become a major component of the rock industry. Punk rock, on the other hand, stripped rock down to a couple of guitar chords, a deliberate and driving rhythm, and insistent vocals. The guitars used heavy distortion, and the drums were loud and fast. Punk also had the energy of bored and restless youth. American journalist Tom Carson describes the Clash's self-titled album:

[It is] a documentary of rock'n'roll teenagers battling first for good times and then for survival in a blasted urban landscape. The Clash's debut album . . . had an astonishing immediacy. You got the feeling that it was recorded virtually in the street, while the National Front marched and the threat of riots flickered all around. . . . Perhaps more than any album ever made, The Clash dramatized rock'n'roll as a last, defiantly cheerful grab for life, something scrawled on the run on subway walls."

Quoted in Steven Wells, *Punk: Young, Loud & Snotty* Thunder's Mouth, New York, 2004, p. 29.

Mick Jones (right) and Joe Strummer perform onstage with The Clash.

adopted the style and sold it in his clothing shop in London. Some kids took the safety-pin ethic a step further and pierced their lips and ears with safety pins. Hell later described his interest in punk rock music and style:

> One thing I wanted to bring back to rock 'n' roll was the knowledge that you invent yourself. . . . That's why I changed my name, why I did all the clothing style things, haircut, everything . . . that is the ultimate message of the New Wave [a term that is often used interchangeably with punk rock]: if you amass the courage that is necessary, you can completely invent yourself.[6]

Angry and Bored in Britain

The first New York punk rockers, such as the Ramones, the New York Dolls, and Television, were the bands responsible for creating the punk sound and look, but it was Britain's punks who would bring punk music to the attention of mainstream America. New York punk gained a small and loyal following in the United States, but it did not get much attention from the American public or the mainstream media. Despite the lack of media attention, many bands continued to make records, and some even embarked on small tours. Some of these tours visited England in the mid-1970's.

Britain's youth connected with the New York punk bands, especially the Ramones. The band's self-titled debut was one of the only punk records available to London's early punks. Many early British punk musicians learned to play instruments by playing along with the record. The arrangements were easy to learn in comparison to the relatively challenging chord structure found in popular rock music.

The aggressive sound of bands like the Ramones also appealed to British youth. They adopted the punk sound and used it as a response to the hopelessness and anger they felt about the sociopolitical environment in Britain during the seventies. Many of these punks were coming of age during great industrial unrest. A miner's strike in 1973–1974 and an Arab oil embargo around the same time limited production in England's factories. A lagging economy and high inflation rates made it difficult for many young people to find employment. A conservative government was in place at the time, and many youth felt they had no chance to influence political change. This fueled a belief among young people that they lacked a future, and the despair resulted in a pessimistic and harsh outlook on life. Punk rock music became one outlet for expressing their discontent with society. This sense of doom is captured in the Sex Pistols' song "No Future" and The Clash's "London's Burning."

Punk was also a response to the boredom that many young people felt in their lives and how radio-friendly rock and roll had lost touch with those who

Thanks to touring, American punk bands like the Ramones established international fan bases in markets like London, England.

no longer believed the 1960s ideals of love and psychedelia were the solution to the world's problems. Steve Diggle of the Buzzcocks, a British punk group, describes why punk proved to be the remedy to the boredom he felt:

The thing was, the musical landscape was dead. There was really nothing happening, and nothing relevant to the modern world. I mean it was 1976 when we started, and the progressive rock bands like Yes and Emerson, Lake, and Palmer were all sounding tired, and seemed to have run their course. They were singing about mushrooms in the sky and whatnot, and we were coming up to a million unemployed in this country [Britain]—which was a first—and there was no excitement anywhere. We were 20 then, and we needed to question our lives, and make music that was relevant to our lives.[7]

The Most Notorious Band

Many of Britain's youth turned to punk rock to create music that was relevant to them, including one of Britain's most notorious punk bands, the Sex Pistols. The Sex Pistols would solidify the rebellious attitude that became associated with punk rock. The band formed in 1975 after hearing the Ramones play in London, and it was not long after that it developed a strong cult following due to its outra-

Identifying with the Audience

Audience participation and identification helped shape the punk rock movement. Punk bands believed that anyone of like mind and attitude could be in a band. The Mekons, a punk band from Leeds, England, included the audience in many of its shows. For example, at one show in 1977 the Mekons led the audience on stage while the band played to it from the viewing floor. The band also emphasized an anti–rock star stance by declaring that anyone who went to its show was considered one of the band members. To create a unifying identity among the band members, the Mekons refused to be called by their last names and instead went by the last name of Mekon.

geous behavior. For example, a live television appearance in 1976 brought the band its first national exposure. Upset with one of the comments made by the host of the *Today* program, lead singer Johnny Rotten and guitarist Steve Jones swore on camera during the live taping. The tabloid press went wild, and the band topped the headlines. The incident caused many problems for the Sex Pistols during its Anarchy Tour to promote its single "Anarchy in the UK." Local authorities canceled many of the Sex Pistols' concerts, and the press gave negative reviews for the rest. Some of the shows ended in riots. In another incident the band played "God Save the Queen" (a song about the queen of England) from London's Thames River while following the queen's motorcade during the Royal Silver Jubilee celebration. They were arrested shortly after.

The Sex Pistols had a handful of singles and only one album in its two-year career. However, the band's ill-mannered behavior helped its music reach a generation of young people who identified with the rebellious attitude. The young punks' rejection of what they saw as bland, conformist society under the grips of an uncaring government held the youth together as much as the music. Joe Strummer of The Clash explains, "We're not going to go quietly to our deaths into some retirement home, eating prozac. This is what they're [the leaders of society] planning for us, unless we do something about it. To always be a punk rocker is something everyone can do. And I mean that by attitude. Attitude!"[8]

Punk music encouraged its listeners to be strong-minded and independent. This mentality provided the backbone to punk music, which helped shape the early independent music movement. Steve Diggle of the Buzzcocks talks about how punk taught him to be independent:

It's given me strength not to be frightened of things in the world, you know? Punk gave me the strength to think, "Yeah, you can stand up and be counted, and do want you want in life, and not be hoodwinked by it all," in a simple, very general sweeping way. It gives you a sense to question things, and be positive, and open up. And that's what it's done for me, to realize you don't have to worry about people in power in society—in terms of how they can pressurize you and steer you in ways. It's made me fearless.[9]

Paving the Way

By the end of the 1970s, the punk movement was firmly established both in England and the United States. Punk offered an alternative to those youth who were bored with the current commercial culture or those who did not fit in or want to fit in with popular society. Punk also provided a means of personal empowerment and introduced young people to the idea of

Frontman Johnny Rotten screams at the audience as the Sex Pistols play their first American concert in Atlanta, Georgia.

making music on their own terms. Whether it is the raucous sound, the wild stage antics, or the political messages, the bands of the underground and punk rock era contributed to the ideology and spirit of future alternative rock movements, including indie rock. By going underground and defying the norm and social conventions, these underground and punk musicians inspired youngsters to experiment and start bands of their own. The punk attitude would also inspire a new mode of distribution through independent record labels. Punk opened up the idea that a major record label was not necessary to make music—you could do it yourself.

Chapter Two

A Do-It-Yourself Mentality

In the spring of 1979 an unknown London punk rock band by the name of the Homosexuals released its first self-recorded single, titled *Hearts in Exile/Soft South Africans*, on its own Black Noise record label. Despite being unheard-of by the mainstream music press, the band sold fifteen hundred of the two thousand copies of the single in two days. It did not advertise, it did not supply press handouts, and it did not send review copies to record labels and fanzines. The band's music was not even played on the radio. Yet the band was able—without the help of the mainstream music industry—to produce a relatively successful single.

The Homosexuals were part of the burgeoning independent punk rock movement during the middle to late 1970s that promoted a do-it-yourself (DIY) ethic. Bands like the Sex Pistols and The Clash popularized punk rock with their antiestablishment and rebellious attitudes and showed people that anyone could be in a band, regardless of musical training. Bands like the Homosexuals, however, took the independent spirit of punk rock further by producing their own records. These bands could play the music they wanted, and they did not have to rely on a record label to distribute or sell their music. By taking control of the recording process, these DIYers showed that anybody who wanted to record an album could.

Recording independently was not entirely new. Garage bands had been making independent recordings since the 1960s, and there had been independent record labels since the beginning of the rock-and-roll movement. However, the independent label scene experienced a lull as the major labels swallowed them up in the late 1960s and early 1970s. As Britain's youth became disenchanted with the corporate hold on the recording industry, they looked back to the days of independent labels as an alternative to signing with a major label. Suddenly kids all over Britain began making their own records.

Once the British punks demystified the recording process, American youth began forming their own small scenes built on the same grassroots DIY principles. In fact, DIY would become the foundation for the indie rock movement that would take place a couple of decades later. Some indie rock musicians today still adhere to the DIY ethic established by their predecessors.

Early Indie Record Labels

When the recording industry began to grow with the increasing popularity of rock and roll in the 1950s, it became diversified. There were plenty of record labels for artists to choose from, and the labels were owned by a lot of different people with different tastes. This meant a variety of choices were available to musicians, and they could choose a label that best suited their personal and artistic interests. The distribution industry (through which records were made available to the people) was mostly independent too, so record companies could easily find eager distributors waiting to ship new products to the stores.

Through the 1950s and 1960s, then, it was relatively easy for an untested band to be signed by one of the many small independent record labels. By the 1970s, however, the biggest record labels desired more control over the industry and began to look for ways to eliminate the competition. By the end of the decade, the major labels made distribution deals with some of the in-

The Sex Pistols pose outside Buckingham Palace as they sign a copy of a new contract with a major recording label.

dependent labels. In other cases they started buying the independent labels outright. They also pumped a lot of money into promotion and advertising to overpower the independent competition and drove them out of business. They were largely able to do so because they had the financial power.

In the 1970s and 1980s the music business was saturated with music from just five or six major labels. Many of these labels recorded similar-sounding bands to compete with each other. It became difficult for bands to get a recording contract if they did not fit the mold. But it was precisely the lack of opportunities for those interested in alternative styles of music that led to the rebirth of the independent record label movement in the late 1970s and early 1980s. Whereas some labels were started by record store owners, others were formed by music fans; still others were started by the musicians and artists themselves. The artists and bands that created or produced music on these labels were considered to be part of an independent or alternative music scene. They either rejected the mainstream record business or were rejected by it and wanted to provide ways for musicians and artists to be heard.

Buzzcocks and Bicycles

By the late 1970s many of Britain's punks were fed up with the limited opportunities within the record industry. Many bands and artists felt rejected by the mainstream record industry, and

they decided to take control of their own record distribution. The Buzzcocks and the Desperate Bicycles were the first two punk bands to make a record without the help of a major recording label. The Buzzcocks, a relatively inexperienced band, formed in Manchester, England, in 1976 after seeing the Sex Pistols in concert earlier that year. Within a matter of months the band produced and released a four-track album entitled *Spiral Scratch* on its New Hormones label. For less than £100 (around $170), the band rented local Indigo Sound Studio and recorded its songs and pressed the result onto vinyl. By February 1977 the band had released the album, which was not only the third U.K. punk record to be issued but also the first independent punk record ever recorded. The band included a breakdown of the costs of the record on the back of the record sleeve to inspire others to act.

Following the Buzzcocks' lead, the Desperate Bicycles, another British band, formed for the sole "purpose of recording and releasing a single on their own label."[10] In fact, the first time vocalist Danny Wigley and keyboardist Nicky Stephens met was when they went into the studio to record their first single, "Smokescreen," in the spring of 1977. The song took three hours to record and cost £153 (roughly $260), which included the cost of pressing five hundred records and producing the sleeves. To cut costs, the band did not

The English band the Buzzcocks produced the first independent punk rock record ever.

record a B-side for its single; instead, it pressed the same song on both sides of the record.

The band sold the singles to small record stores such as Small Wonder and Bonaparte Records and to various independent distributors such as Rough Trade, eventually selling out in four months. With its profits, the band turned around and pressed one thousand more records, which sold out two weeks later. Despite its small success, the band never had the desire to sign with a record company. Wigley comments in the music magazine *New Musical Express* on the Desperate Bicycles' desire to remain independent: "For us it's really important to be independent. We've made a stand, small

as it may be, and we've actually kept independent. *We're* in control of the music and of what we want to do."[11]

DIY Records

The success of the Buzzcocks and the Desperate Bicycles inspired many bands to go out and make their own records. According to writer Bob Stanley, between 1979 and 1981 there were roughly nine hundred DIY singles released. Most of the records had a similar look and were made in a similar way. The sleeves were often handmade photo copies of basic lettering or pictures. Photos of the band were rare. When they did grace a picture sleeve, the band was usually shown at a live show, emphasizing that the band was not a studio creation. Sometimes the photos were blurry or fuzzy in order to represent band unity by not highlighting actual faces or featuring any one member prominently.

Some of the sleeves were just simple brown paper bags with the names of the songs written in marker across the front. In many cases, the sleeves did not even list the full names of the band members. Rather than including a contact address for the band, it was much more common to list pressing plants, printers, and the costs of production calculated down to the last cent. By explaining how a record was made—sometimes with step-by-step instructions—it invited a much wider audience to participate in making music. The DIY ethic stressed that artist and consumer were members of the same scene.

Indie Record Stores

Independent record stores were one of the key elements of the burgeoning indie music scene. They varied in their size and the kind of music they carried—some carried mainstream music along with more obscure music—but they provided an outlet for new music to be heard.

One successful indie record store that helped shape the indie music scene was located in Minneapolis, Minnesota. It was called Oar Folkjokeopus (partly named after an eccentric British folk album by Roy Harper called *Folkjokeopus*). Owned by Vern Sander, a record collector interested in rare and obscure music, the store became, according to the Twin/Tone label Web site, "a clubhouse for musical misfits of all kinds."

Oar Folkjokeopus was the first store in the Midwest to carry hard-to-find imports and indie-label records well before the first punk explosion. The store became the cornerstone of the Minneapolis scene, and various independent club owners would inquire with the store before booking an up-and-coming band. Club owners would want to know what size crowd they should expect, what opening act to feature, and if they should book the show for more than one night. It was just one of the many intimate relationships that took place between artists, clubs, labels, and independent record stores.

Peter Jesperson, "The Twin/Tone Story," Twin/Tone, June 1998. www.twintone.com.

Members of the Rolling Stones flip through a fanzine.

Fanzines

The DIY ethic extended beyond recording into the realm of writing. Fans of the underground bands began making their own fan magazines, or fanzines, to follow the independent music scene. The fanzines were non-professional, often crude publications that included hand-printed text and collaged graphics. The publications were not funded by commercial or public ventures and were produced for minimal costs. Some of the most well-known fanzines at the time were *Sniffin' Glue, Jamming!, London's Outage*, and *Ugly Things*.

The British fanzine *Sniffin' Glue* was started by Mark Perry in July 1976. Working as a bank clerk, Perry was inspired to start a fanzine after failing to find any mainstream publications that discussed punk bands like the Ramones, who were touring England at the time. In a series of twelve issues over the course of a year, he chronicled various punk bands and concerts. In his first issue Perry reviewed two Ramones shows in London as well as the exploits of other bands such as Blue Oyster Cult. Throughout the fanzine, Perry championed the DIY ethic. In one issue in 1977 he included drawings of three chord patterns with the caption "this is a chord, this is another, this is a third. Now form a band."[12]

The first issues of *Sniffin' Glue* only sold about fifty copies, but before the year was over, the circulation had increased to fifteen thousand. Though the fanzine was popular amongst punk rockers, Perry feared that it would become popular in the mainstream and ceased publication after a single year. To keep the DIY spirit alive, however, in his last issues he encouraged others to create their own fanzines. Many did.

Indie Record Labels

Independent record labels sprang up at the same time as the fanzines. These labels helped bands record as well as distribute their music. Some of the more well-known indie record labels were Illegal, Deptford Fun City, Step Forward, Small Wonder, and Rough Trade. The latter was one of the most successful independent labels. Rough Trade grew out of a successful record store of the same name in 1978. Founder Geoff Travis had an eclectic musical taste and signed a wide variety of bands, including Stiff Little Fingers, the Slits, Pere Ubu, Scritti Politti, and the Smiths.

Rough Trade was considered the most radical of the small labels. The label incorporated the idea of equality in all aspects of business. The company was run like a co-op, with all workers receiving an equal amount of pay. Furthermore, it shunned all corporate business practices prevalent in the music industry. It avoided the glossy marketing campaigns that were common with the large labels and the seventies rock bands they signed, such as Led Zeppelin and Pink Floyd. Rough Trade also did not rely on creating relationships with radio stations and large music retailers to create a fan base. Instead, it built relationships with musicians, independent record stores, and fanzines in order to gain exposure and sell music. Rough Trade showed that big budgets and expensive recording techniques were not necessary to sell a record, let alone record one. And, more importantly, the label worked to protect the artistic integrity of the musicians and did not compromise the artists' sound or intent in order to sell product.

As a small record label, Rough Trade also operated as an independent distributor. It helped bands that had recorded their own singles or albums secure a distribution channel, usually through a network of local, independently owned record shops. Rough Trade also signed contracts with bands on a record-by-record basis instead of tying a band into a multi-album deal in which the pressures to produce product often forced creativity to take

The Rough Trade indie record label signed a variety of talent, including the Smiths (pictured).

the backseat. Furthermore, all profits were split equally between the band and the label.

Although many of these records were made for local distribution, copies of the records made their way through small underground music scenes in places like Tokyo, Stockholm, San Francisco, Los Angeles, and Washington, D.C. In 1978 *Zigzag* magazine cataloged 231 independent labels; this included large and small labels as well as a wide array of genres, including rock and roll, reggae, and punk. But by 1980 the number had jumped to more than 800 due to the influx of punk labels.

American DIY

The success of the independent British music scene inspired American youth to adopt a DIY mentality. As Britain's independent punk records made their way across the Atlantic, American youth saw that they, too, could record their own music without the help of a major record label.

In cities across America (Washington, D.C.; Minneapolis; and Los Angeles), small scenes were forming independently of one another, but all were influenced by the early American punk bands and the British punk scene. The sound of music most associated with the American underground scene in the early 1980s was called hardcore. Hardcore was a heavier, faster version of punk.

Following the British lead, local American bands and music fans created an extensive underground network that included college radio stations, fanzines, local cable-access shows, nightclubs, and independent record stores. Some of the more popular fanzines were *Flipside*, *Maximumrocknroll*, and *Forced Exposure*, but there were hundreds of others, most of them photocopied and stapled together. The art work that appeared in fanzines often consisted of photocopied collages with scrawled writing. Some of the record labels also featured such primitive images.

Some of the most popular American indie record labels included SST, Dischord, Touch & Go, and Sub Pop, and these gained a large roster of artists. However, there were countless other labels that made significant contributions, including Alternative Tentacles, Taang!, Frontier, Slash, and Wax Trax. These labels built unique identities by creating particular aesthetics in their music, album art, and catalog copy.

Young people—mostly college students and social outcasts—were what allowed the scene to thrive. Small scenes in urban centers and college towns fostered unity among the likeminded. Young people wanted to see local bands and their friends' bands play rather than some of the popular mainstream acts. Indie bands believed that it was easier to relate to the audience without the overblown gimmicks of mainstream rock acts. Author Michael Azzerad describes the virtues of independent music:

Instructions Included!

Punk band Scritti Politti listened to the Desperate Bicycles' invitation to go out and make a record. In 1978 it released its first single, titled Skank Bloc Bologna, *which it packaged in a sleeve that contained the details of the recording and the costs. The sleeve read:*

Recording: Space Studios @ 19 Victoria Street, Cambridge. £98.00 for 14 hours, master tape included. Mastering: Pye London Studios @ 17 Great Cumberland Place, London W1 - IBC (George) Sound Recording Studios @ 35 Portland Place, London W1. £40.00 for cutting of lacquer from master tape. Pressing: PYE Records (Sales) Ltd. @ Western Road, Mitcham, Surrey. £369.36 for 2,500 copies at 13p [pence], £27.00 for processing (electro plating of lacquer). Labels: E.G. Rubber Stamps, 28 Bridge Street, Hitchin, Herts. £8.00 for rubber stamp on white labels (labels included in cost of pressing).

Quoted in Richard Mason, "'No More Time for Spectating' or How the Desperate Bicycles & Scritti Politti Didn't Quite Manage to Conquer the Known Universe in the Late '70s," November 1999. www.furious.com/perfect/scritti.html

British punk band Scritti Politti independently released its first single.

Corporate rock was about living larger; indie was about living realistically and being proud of it. Indie bands didn't need million-dollar promotional budgets and multiple costume changes. All they needed was to believe in themselves and for a few other people to believe in them, too. You didn't need some big corporation to fund you, or even verify that you were any good. It was about viewing as a virtue what most saw as a limitation.[13]

And this "virtue" became a badge of honor that drew more people to the independent scene.

SST and Dischord

Since hardcore was never marketable to major labels, many bands chose to start their own record labels. Black Flag's Greg Ginn launched the first independent hardcore label, SST, when no other record company would listen to his band. When Ginn created SST, people became aware that there were other hardcore scenes in America. Until then, most bands thought that their local scene was the only place where they could hear or play hardcore music. Shortly after the formation of SST, Ian McKaye of Minor Threat created Dischord Records in Washington, D.C. These labels would become two of the defining indie labels in the 1980s.

SST and Dischord operated with a sense of community for their fellow hardcore musicians. However, they also ran their companies with a strong business sense. They sent album promos of their artists to rock critics, and they made sure that their artists were

Black Flag vocalist Henry Rollins dives into a concert crowd. Greg Ginn of Black Flag launched the first independent hardcore record label, SST.

Some indie rock bands continue to follow the touring paths originally blazed by early hardcore groups.

represented in the ads of all the major fanzines. Like many other independent labels, they signed bands on an album-by-album basis. That way, a band was not locked into three- or five-album contracts, and they had the freedom to change labels after each album. The goal of Dischord was to own its own music and not give up its rights or the money it earned to the big record companies. The label wanted the music to be accessible to as many people as possible. It limited the price of CDs to ten dollars and concert tickets were often five dollars. Both Dischord and SST did not follow traditional music business practices. Instead, the labels operated out of necessity and learned as they went along. They made most of their decisions—such as pricing—based on their own identification with

their audiences. They were young fans as well as entrepreneurs.

Carving a Path

Touring was one of the ways hardcore bands could find interested listeners. Many of the early American hardcore bands created a touring path that would be emulated by future indie rock bands as a standard way of promoting their music. College radio was in its infancy, so it was almost impossible for a punk or hardcore band to gain a national following unless it toured. Most big acts traditionally put out an album and then toured to promote it. However, hardcore bands often toured first and then put out a record.

Bands often worked together, sharing news of venues that welcomed hardcore music. Musicians would introduce each other to owners of venues, or all the bands from one record label might gain access to a certain club. Independent record labels would also support tours. McKaye of Dischord Records networked with others in the indie scene. He called customers who bought their CD through mail order, radio stations, and record stores, and he asked these interested listeners where the bands should play. By creating a network of partnerships, the early hardcore bands created a touring path across America. By the mid-1980s there was an established pattern to making indie music: tour first, then record, and then release a record.

The Hardcore Scene Splits

Initially the hardcore scene was built on unity, and all the bands were very supportive of each other. Eventually, though, some of the small labels began to grow in size and become more popular. Some indie bands like Hüsker Dü and the Replacements also began getting airplay on college radio and grew beyond their indie roots. Many bands welcomed the attention and seized the opportunity to sign a recording contract with a larger label to obtain more money and increased exposure. Others in the scene considered those bands who signed with majors to be sellouts. The indie movement split into factions, and the scene began to dissolve during the mid-1980s. According to Black Flag's Greg Ginn, hardcore fell apart when "people started seeing money in indy rock and . . . we couldn't go out on a limb anymore."[14]

The DIY aesthetic remained with those bands that did not sign with a major label. By the mid-1980s, however, the emphasis began to shift to college radio. Suddenly a band's chances to be heard increased exponentially. The alternative bands on college radio played much more diverse-sounding music than just punk and hardcore.

Chapter Three

College Rock

During the middle to late 1980s, underground music began to get a lot of airplay on college radio stations. College radio provided an alternative to mainstream radio, which mostly played similar-sounding Top 40 music. College radio was crucial in the development of alternative music because it exposed fans to independent music from across the nation. No longer did fans have to wait for new music that arrived via touring bands, like in the early hardcore days; instead, they could hear new music from bands as soon as it was released. The music of bands that were played on college radio was eventually referred to as college rock since college radio was the main source of alternative music at the time.

College radio playlists moved beyond the punk and hardcore sounds that had characterized much of the independent music from the late 1970s and early 1980s and included a variety of music from American bands such as Sonic Youth, the Pixies, and Dinosaur Jr. to British postpunk acts like the Smiths, the Cure, and Siouxsie and the Banshees. The music played on college radio was part of a network of like-minded college students. No longer were these kids the disaffected youth of the punk and hardcore scene; they were educated, privileged, and had money to spend. However, like punk and hardcore, college rock was a youth music that hinged upon audience identification. The bands and the fans were all part of the same circle. College rock narrowed the gap between the performer and audience and made the music seem more personal. Writer Hugo Lindgren describes why he found college rock so appealing:

> I was in college when the category known as "college rock" was popularized, and though it was as much a marketing conceit as anything else, I bought the concept immediately. The Replacements

and Husker Du, the Blake Babies, the Pixies, and Pavement: These bands weren't just my idols, they felt like my peers, and a good part of the pleasure I took in their music was imagining that there wasn't much that separated me from them. Like the earliest punks, they made a virtue of their amateurism, of starting things without knowing where they'd end. And for someone like me, on the scary precipice of adulthood, that was an incredibly exciting fantasy: the notion that sheer guts, plus a willingness to bare your weaknesses (no vocal talent necessary!), could make you into a rock star.[15]

College radio became associated with independent or alternative music and greatly influenced the development of indie rock in the late 1990s. Most emerging indie rock musicians relied on college radio to gain exposure and build their fan bases. In fact, many indie rock bands became established via a network of college radio stations.

The Rise of College Radio

Prior to the rise of college radio, most rock music fans listened to rock on commercial radio stations located on the FM spectrum. In the 1970s commercial radio became a profitable market, with large music stations making quite a bit of money. Large corporations took notice of the booming market and started buying and creating new radio stations. By the mid-1980s some twelve thousand commercial stations vied for audiences. As a result, the market was incredibly fragmented, with each station playing to a small niche; soft hits, oldies, new rock, disco, and Latino rock were some of the popular formats. During the mid-1980s, however, hard-rock music (played by bands such as Poison, Warrant, and Mötley Crüe) dominated the FM radio stations that played a "classic-rock" format.

Although there was no shortage of rock radio stations, most of the stations were playing the same music from the same bands. Many young music fans became increasingly bored with the hard-rock format and longed to hear new music with which they could identify. Many of these fans tuned in to local college radio stations to hear the alternative music that they could not hear on commercial radio. Rachel Bloch, rock director at WSRN at Swarthmore College, describes the importance of college radio stations in offering an alternative to mainstream music: "The point is not to get lots of listeners. It's to support independent music, to give students experience in radio, and to expose those who care to [hear] music that they would have a hard time finding otherwise."[16]

College radio stations were located on college campuses and were operated and run by college students. The stations were mostly small, occupied a narrow bandwidth on the radio spectrum, and usually had low wattage. As

The British band the Cure was one of many postpunk acts that influenced the music played on college radio in the early 1980s.

a result, college stations did not have a great range, and most of the people tuning in were students. However, college radio exposed these local fans to underground music from around the country. People had an opportunity to hear bands that might not have played shows in their hometowns. Some of the earliest college radio stations that embraced alternative music were WXCI in Danbury, Connecticut; WPRB in Princeton, New Jersey; and Brown University's WBRU in Provi-

dence, Rhode Island. WPRB disc jockey Jon Solomon had an alternative music show as early as 1986.

Most college stations operated with noncommercial licenses. This meant they had a lot of freedom to play whatever kind of music they wanted because they were not beholden to advertisers. Douglas Wolk, a former managing editor of *CMJ New Music Monthly*, explains why college radio stations had more freedom than commercial radio stations: "The most important thing about college radio stations is that they're not commercial—they don't need to run with ad sales in mind. College radio's mandate, then, is to provide programming that is thoughtful and daring."[17]

College radio introduced college students to underground bands like the Pixies, the Cocteau Twins, and Elephant 6. Many of these underground rock bands had been influenced by the punk bands of the 1970s and were experimental in their sound and songwriting. This appealed to the college music fans because it provided something new and an alternative to the classic rock music with which they had grown bored.

A Shift in Sound

In the mid-1980s college rock broadened its sound beyond the hard-edged bands like the Minutemen, Black Flag, and Minor Threat as bands began to experiment with new instruments. Some bands began to incorporate Casio keyboards, which could produce unique sounds that a guitar, bass, or drums could not. Other bands created a quieter guitar sound by decreasing the amount of distortion that typically had been used in the hardcore scene

College radio helped introduce underground bands like the Pixies (pictured) to wider audiences.

The John Peel Sessions

Throughout radio's history, numerous radio disc jockeys (DJs) have single-handedly changed the careers of various alternative rock bands and musicians by playing their music on the radio. One of the most respected and longest-lasting was British DJ and broadcaster John Peel. Beginning in 1967, Peel hosted a show on Radio 1, the new pop music station on the British Broadcasting Corporation (BBC). He soon became a popular fixture, and thousands of listeners tuned in to hear his shows.

One of his trademarks was the development of the John Peel Sessions. These sessions included performances by bands that prerecorded four songs at the BBC's studios, which were then exclusively played on Peel's show. He had an eclectic and avant-garde taste in music and showcased new music to his listeners. He became a strong advocate of the punk-rock movement and any independent music that followed. Peel's support helped launch the careers of several indie musicians during the 1980s, including the Cure, the Wedding Present, and the Smiths.

Peel's Radio 1 show lasted thirty-seven years and ended with his death in 2004. More than two thousand artists had recorded four thousand sessions with him over the years.

and by creating a more melodic pop sound. Some bands even began to embrace some traditionally mainstream rock practices because it was an alternative to some of the conventions becoming established in punk and hardcore. For example, bands such as Dinosaur Jr. and Sebadoh often incorporated extended guitar solos and "soaring" melodies, which were components that punks had rejected earlier.

In addition to experimenting with sound, many bands began to focus on lyrics. The lyrics of many college rock bands often referred to art, literature, and philosophy—topics many artists had studied in college. For instance, the college rock band REM wrote obscure lyrics tinted with artistic references. Other bands wrote introspective lyrics (though many of the early hardcore bands would consider themselves introspective) that questioned themselves on a personal level instead of questioning society, as many punks had.

The most popular of the college rock bands were the Replacements, REM, the Smiths, and Dinosaur Jr.

However, college rock also embraced some mainstream acts, including U2, Peter Gabriel, and Sting. They were considered part of the college rock genre because they wrote songs about social issues, which appealed to many students on college campuses.

The Pixies was one of college rock's most influential bands during the middle-to-late 1980s due to its willingness to experiment. The Pixies formed in Massachusetts in 1986 and included Black Francis and Kim Deal as dual singer-songwriters. Many bands at the time played a distinctive style of music that was easily classified as a certain musical genre. The Pixies, however, ignored musical classifications and incorporated any number of musical styles into its songs. The band sometimes combined layered guitar distortion with simple folk rock harmonies. Underlying its experimental sound was a dark and foreboding rhythm. Although the band was liked by critics, for most of its career it received little airplay outside college radio. In 1989 the Pixies released *Doolittle* on a major label, and for a short time it experienced some mainstream attention. Despite this, the band mostly remained in the underground circuit and toured successfully for a couple of years until it split up in 1991.

Indie Music Charts

At first college rock had a mostly underground following of students interested in independent music. The music began to gain momentum, however, as these college rock bands traveled through college rock towns. Many of the students who worked at the college radio stations naturally attended a lot of shows and were constantly exposed to new music. In turn, they would play these bands on their radio shows. The record industry soon began to take notice of the small successes independent bands were having on college radio.

One of the reasons why the record industry began to pay attention to college rock was because it was the first independent music to make ripples on the music charts. Two bands that helped bring independent music onto the music charts were New Order and

Lead singer Morrissey performs with the Smiths.

the Smiths. The Smiths, known for its gloomy lyrics and downbeat pop sound, was a British band that had much success on the record charts despite being signed to an independent label. It was signed to Rough Trade, and its 1984 self-titled debut entered the U.K. charts at number two. Its song "Heaven Knows I'm Miserable Now" reached number ten on the U.K singles charts. The band's second album, *Meat Is Murder*, landed at the top of the U.K. charts within the first week of its release. These chart successes brought some mainstream attention to the variety of music that was escaping major label notice.

I Want My MTV

While college radio had provided the main source for alternative music throughout the 1980s, the record industry was looking for other ways to penetrate the youth market. The birth of MTV (Music Television) in 1981 would provide mass audiences a chance not only to hear new music but also to see the artists who were producing the music. This worked to further audience identification between artists and their fans.

MTV started out as a northern New Jersey cable show that offered music videos in a low-cost program format. Initially, record labels provided the videos for free as a form of advertising. The show quickly expanded nationwide, and bands from all over the country (and even foreign bands) suddenly had visibility. Videos had the power to make an unknown band popular in a very short time. Bands that previously had not received radio airplay could be featured on MTV. In many cases, MTV could launch a band's career.

By the mid-1980s MTV—like mainstream radio—was dominated by Top 40 music. The programmers at the network, however, realized that they could tap other audiences by expanding the type of music MTV played. In 1986, around the time college rock had started to gain mainstream attention, the show *120 Minutes* was created to feature alternative music. The two-hour-long show was aired from 1986 to 2003 (first on MTV and then on MTV2) and played videos from artists like the Ramones, Morrissey, and Hüsker Dü. MTV was important to alternative music because it essentially exposed greater numbers of people to alternative rock. It invited kids who were not part of the college radio scene to hear and see alternative music.

College Rock Graduates

College rock playlists soon began to draw the attention of major radio stations and record labels. They saw how successful independent bands could be and how powerful college radio and MTV were in turning the youth market—the largest portion of the record-buying public—on to new music. Commercial radio began to expand its repertoire, playing bands that formerly resided only on college radio. It was another step in bringing some of the more accessible college rock music into the mainstream. For instance, WFNX, a commercial station in Boston, Massachusetts, began playing college rock by the end of the 1980s. As a result, many larger labels began to sign some of the popular college rock bands, including Hüsker Dü, the Replacements, and REM.

The band members of REM were the so-called college rock gods of the mid-1980s. Formed at the University of Georgia in Athens in 1980, they gained most of their fan base from college radio stations. They also won a lot of critical success for combining punk and folk influences with enig-matic lyrics to create what many critics have described as jangly guitar-pop. They played small clubs and kept a low-key image for many years. However, due to REM's popularity on college radio, the band began selling out twelve-thousand-seat venues.

By 1987 the band had produced four albums on the small IRS label. All of the albums had gone gold. Shortly after completing the album *Document* in 1987, the band signed with Warner Brothers. Warner Brothers advertised and promoted the band, and suddenly the REM sound and format was known by mainstream audiences around the world. Many of the band's songs topped the popular-music

REM moved from humble, independent beginnings to selling out massive concert venues worldwide.

A Cassette Culture

One of the offshoots of the DIY ethic of punk that occurred at the same time that college rock was in full swing was the home recording of compact audio cassettes. Bands often recorded themselves on tape at home and then passed the tapes on to friends or distributed them through independent labels. The tapes were also sold via mail order or were exchanged in a loose network of independent labels and fanzines. Some bands would copy their music after being sent a blank tape and a self-addressed envelope. It was a popular way for indie musicians to distribute their music.

The cassette-tape movement was first popular in Britain during the postpunk period from 1978 to 1984. In the United States, however, the trend occurred during the middle to late 1980s (and even into the 1990s), after *New Musical Express,* a weekly U.K. music magazine, released a compilation called *C-86* in 1986. The compilation was released on cassette tape and was available through mail order. It included bands such as Primal Scream, the Bodines, and the Pastels.

---

charts. The band struggled with how to proceed in terms of its music once more people were listening to its songs. For instance, singer Michael Stipe was known for mumbling hard-to-understand lyrics. Once REM became more visible, Stipe wondered if the band should adjust its sound to satisfy its new audience. He explained in a 1987 interview, "There's a little more weight on my shoulders as far as what I say. . . . I guess I've figured out that I can't just blabber anything I want to anymore, which I've done before, though not a great deal. On some of the earlier songs, whatever I happened to be singing, we recorded it."[18]

Many bands, including REM, experienced the problems that resulted from the crossover success of alternative rock in the mainstream pop world—a problem that exists for some artists even today. When a band reaches the mainstream, it has a much larger audience. Original fans of the band—when the band was relatively unknown—feel less special if they are one of a hundred thousand listeners. Some of these fans accuse the band of selling out and surrendering their indie credentials. This cultish set of fans believes indie bands lose their integrity and often their uniqueness if they try to please mass audiences. Lou Barlow, lead singer of one of the quintessential college rock bands, Sebadoh, comments on forsaking the band's "indie cred" to simply play music. "It seems like a misnomer. It's not really important to us, and we're not going to cater to people's personal politics." Instead the band prefers that its music reaches more than a fanzine editor who gets upset when his or her favorite band goes mainstream. Barlow continues, "If you record and put something out, you should be prepared for the idea that maybe more than one person will wanna listen to it. And then you have to accept the fact that that could be a million or two million. Or whatever. It's all the same to me."[19]

Regardless of whether a band remained popular on the indie circuit or made it to the mainstream, college radio was an important tool for any band to gain exposure and be heard by its peers. It would remain the dominant way for an unknown band to have its music played. Although the college rock sound of the 1980s would recede into the background, a new sound would take its place. College radio was constantly renewing itself by playing the next underground music. College towns around America began to embrace local bands again, as the majority of the bands that had once been popular began to enter the mainstream. By the early 1990s college radio was ready to birth the next alternative rock music—grunge.

Chapter Four

The Selling of Grunge Music

For most of its history, alternative music remained an underground music, with the exception of a few college rock bands that graduated to major-label and commercial success. In the early 1990s, however, one band, Nirvana, would forever break down the barrier between alternative and mainstream when its album *Nevermind* was released. The album's first single, "Smells Like Teen Spirit," had a brash yet melodic guitar sound coupled with lyrics about the vapidity of youth culture. It was a tonic to bored teenagers and twenty-somethings who were disenchanted with the tired reign of glammed-up heavy metal bands that belted out clichéd tunes about having a good time. "Smells Like Teen Spirit" also had its own video, which was made on a shoestring budget and displayed a band devoid of makeup, special effects, or gimmicks. The video brought instant attention to Nirvana, and almost overnight the band became known across America.

The success of Nirvana drew attention to its home state of Washington, where several other bands seemed to be playing a similar sound and sporting a similar non–rock star appearance. Emphasizing the hard-rock sound and unkempt look of the bands, critics dubbed the music and the scene *grunge*.

Grunge soon dominated the airwaves, and many of these alternative bands that were used to playing small venues in front of friends were suddenly embarking on major tours, playing in front of increasingly larger audiences, and being signed by major labels. Like all "scenes," grunge was quickly co-opted and sold, becoming more of a marketing term used to sell youth culture to the masses than a distinct genre of music. Major labels had finally figured out how to cash in on alternative culture.

An Isolated Scene

Around 1985 an alternative music scene was starting to take root in the

Seattle area, including Aberdeen, an isolated logging town located midway up the Pacific coast in Washington State. Aberdeen was a depressed town economically, especially after automation in the logging industry had created a high rate of unemployment. According to Kurt Cobain, lead singer and guitarist for Nirvana, Aberdeen was "totally secluded from any culture at all . . . [there was] nothing but rednecks and guns and booze."[20]

Aberdeen, like Seattle, experiences heavy rainfall most of the year. As a result, people typically stayed inside, and the area youth often chose to play music to fight their boredom. Cobain describes how he created his own punk music since such music was not accessible in Aberdeen:

The Sex Pistols, the Buzzcocks, any 'seventy-seven [1977] punk rock band was totally influential to our music. But it was almost impossible to get exposed to English punk. We only had one radio station, a soft rock AM station. I remember being about fourteen and having a subscription to *Creem* magazine and I would read about the Sex Pistols, but I never got to hear anything. . . . I decided to create my own punk rock with my electric guitar.[21]

At the time, there was not much of a live music scene. Seattle was not a town through which bands toured—most bands went only as far north as San Francisco. However, there were two or three venues to hear live local music, including the Showbox and the Gorilla Room/Garden. If a band wanted to put on a show, band members would do all the work themselves—rent a hall, take tickets, and even clean up afterward.

Bands were not typically concerned with success in Seattle. They were mostly interested in playing music for their friends. According to record producer Jack Endino, "Nobody was too worried about success because we were living in Seattle. It wasn't LA [Los Angeles]. Nobody was gonna come sign us."[22]

The Seattle Sound

There was a defining quality that characterized most of the music being created in Seattle. Many bands were influenced by the punk rock and hardcore music of the early 1980s bands, as well as classic hard-rock bands such as Aerosmith. Yet these garage bands reinvented punk by adding incredible amounts of guitar distortion to make a "fuzzy" sound. The sound was then amplified to incredibly high decibels and was mixed with plenty of feedback. It was what one *Newsweek* writer once termed "a wall of white noise."[23] Former bass player for Guns n' Roses Duff McKagan describes the sound that came from Seattle: "You gotta understand Seattle, its grunge. People are into rock & roll and into noise, and they're building airplanes all the time and there's lots of noise, and there's rain and musty garages.

Nirvana, which included frontman Kurt Cobain and bass guitarist Krist Novoselic, played an instrumental part in establishing Seattle's grunge rock scene.

Musty garages create a certain noise."[24]

The Seattle bands also believed in recording their music as if they were playing a live show. In fancy recordings it is possible for bands to create a richer sound by overlaying tracks on top of one another—sometimes as many as twenty-four tracks. The sound from each track is then separated, edited, and then put back to-gether (this is referred to as remaster-ing). These techniques are often used to create a rich tone and range. How-ever, a band cannot replicate this sound at a live show. Seattle bands avoided these recording tricks, prefer-ring that their recorded sound mimic their live shows. Mudhoney, a suc-cessful band from Seattle, chose to record an album on cheap four-track equipment, despite having the means

Daniel Johnston

Singer-songwriter Daniel Johnston epitomizes the complex relationship between creating indie music while also desiring fame and success. Born in Sacramento, California, in 1961, Johnston has been an artist, filmmaker, and singer-songwriter since his early teens. From a young age he made music in the hope of one day becoming famous. He originally played piano but then switched to guitar after he moved to Austin, Texas. It was at about this time that he began exhibiting signs of bipolar disorder.

Johnston began his career as an independent musician by recording his music on cassettes in his garage using a fifty-nine-dollar Sanyo boombox. He dubbed each tape individually and handcrafted the covers for each cassette by pasting his personal cartoon drawings to the cassette cover. Johnston would then distribute his tapes by hand to newspaper writers, club owners, or anyone who would accept one of them. Johnston eventually played some shows in Austin and gained a cult following by those who were intrigued by his odd behavior but clever and unusual lyrics.

In 1994 Johnston signed with Atlantic Records but was dropped by the major label when his album only sold fifty-four hundred copies. Despite his mainstream failure, he has been a favorite of underground music bands. Close to two hundred artists have recorded covers of his songs, including grunge-rock darlings Pearl Jam. Though in poor health and mentally unstable, Johnston continues to record music and tour internationally.

Daniel Johnston began his career by recording his music with a simple boombox.

to rent a nice studio with multitrack recorders that could clean up any performance.

Sub Pop Records Arrives

In the late eighties, most Seattle bands did not expect to gain the attention of major record labels—that happened in Los Angeles or New York. However, a well-known independent record label named Sub Pop (which had started out as a fanzine in 1980) decided to harness the Seattle sound and promote it as best it could. In 1988 Sub Pop Records released a three-CD boxed set called *Sub Pop 200*. It contained bands such as Soundgarden, Mudhoney, and Nirvana. The set was also sold with a twenty-page booklet filled with photographs capturing long-haired band members wearing flannel shirts, dripping in sweat, frantically playing their guitars. The booklet was responsible for making that image—especially the flannel shirts and unkempt hair—the image of the grunge scene.

Sub Pop went on to record many of Seattle's grunge bands and was the independent record label of choice for many like-minded bands looking to

The Seattle band Mudhoney chose to record their first album using cheap, four-track equipment instead of using a high-priced studio.

record an album. Nirvana, formed in 1987 by high school friends Kurt Cobain and Krist Novoselic, recorded its first album, *Bleach*, on Sub Pop for roughly six hundred dollars. Nirvana went on to record its next album, *Nevermind*, with Sub Pop, even signing a contract with the label. Many local music fans turned to Sub Pop recordings to hear new music. Quite a few bands gained modest followings after appearing on the Sub Pop label.

Despite the small successes of local bands, Sup Pop was not a very stable business and was close to bankruptcy in 1991. Label owners Jonathan Poneman and Bruce Pavitt decided to sell 49 percent interest in the label to Geffen Records for $20 million. (The label was originally a $20,000 investment.) This included the buyout of the remainder of Nirvana's contract with Sub Pop. Poneman and Pavitt were to maintain complete artistic control of the label and would receive 2 percent of the royalties Geffen earned from Nirvana's *Nevermind* album. Following the partial buyout, Geffen went on to market the band with an intensity that underground music had not previously experienced. The label unleashed massive quantities of radio promos to college radio station managers. The band also made the video for its song "Smells Like Teen Spirit," which was placed in heavy rotation on MTV. As a result, Nirvana received much airplay and consequently became a nationally recognized name on college radio.

Overnight Success

Nirvana's album *Nevermind* was released in September 1991 and went gold in a few weeks. It bumped Michael Jackson out of the number-one spot on *Billboard* magazine's al-bum charts. When Nirvana's video for "Smells Like Teen Spirit" appeared in October 1991, it was not long before the band was selling out clubs around the country. By mid-January 1992, *Nevermind* was the number-one album in the United States.

As "Smells Like Teen Spirit" leaped immediately into the mainstream markets, major labels looked to sign any Seattle band they could. Record executives flocked to the city, as did bands hoping to capitalize on the music scene. Because Nirvana had been such a success on college radio, they hyped the Seattle bands to college radio stations, hoping to cash in on the next Nirvana. Like all successful scenes, grunge was soon commoditized and sold as a trendy alternative to pop music. No longer was the emphasis on the music but rather on the look and laid-back atmosphere of grunge. Movies like Cameron Crowe's *Singles* tried to replicate the Seattle music scene, and high-end clothing designers marketed designs that mimicked the slovenly dress of many of the Seattle musicians. Grunge bands appeared on the covers of mainstream music magazines such as *Rolling Stone*. A 1992 cover of the magazine featured Nirvana with the headline "New Faces of Rock."

Nirvana and a number of other Seattle bands dominated the mainstream radio charts for the next five years. Bands like Soundgarden, Pearl Jam, Alice in Chains, Screaming Trees, and Mudhoney not only ushered in a new sound but also swept aside the pop mainstream. By 1994 the seven best-selling Seattle bands generated $200 million in gross revenues for their major labels. The grunge scene (which also came to embrace bands outside of Seattle that had a similar sound) dominated MTV and some music charts. Grunge was no longer a local outsider scene, it was a defining fixture of the mainstream music industry.

Not everyone was thrilled about the success of grunge music. Most of the bands had no idea how the mainstream music industry worked, and many were surprised at the level of fame that came along with signing with a major label. Bassist Kim Thalil of Soundgarden comments, "Kinda figured we'd play guitar or drums . . . sing . . . make a record, play a show. People like your record, and they like your show. . . . [We] couldn't really anticipate it becoming interviews, videos and photo sessions. In the forefront of our minds we sort of knew that these were things that went along with the job but you never really can anticipate it until you are there. We can do without the fame stuff."[25]

Nirvana poses underwater in a swimming pool during a promotional photo shoot for the Nevermind *album.*

Riot Grrrl

The Riot Grrl movement sprouted in the early nineties as a response to the male-dominated grunge music scene. It was loud, fast, and angry-sounding rock music played by women. Riot Grrrl music focused on anger and aggressiveness rather than girly cuteness or innocence. It was started by a group of women in Washington, D.C., and Olympia, Washington, who were calling for a feminist revolution in rock music. The slogan that captured their philosophy was "Revolution Girl-Style Now."

Bands like Bratmobile and Bikini Kill were at the forefront of the movement that advocated for all-female bands and female ownership of record labels. Jenny Toomey of the band Tsunami was one participant who took the movement seriously. After becoming frustrated with the mainstream recording industry, Toomey, along with friend Kristen Thompson, formed the record label called the Simple Machines.

Bikini Kill vocalist Kathleen Hannah performs onstage in 1992.

The twosome advocated a do-it-yourself ethic and encouraged women and all independent musicians to be in control of their own businesses. They even wrote and produced a twenty-four-page manual that described the exact process for recording and distributing music independently. The Riot Grrrl movement reached its peak in 1992 and 1993.

The mainstream success of grunge music changed the underground music scene and made it difficult for any alternative band to exist outside of the spotlight. Singer and guitarist Eric Bachmann of Archers of Loaf claims, "It made it impossible for there to be any sort of an underground scene. The minute a band put out a single, the major labels knew about it. People who were doing dishes really hated being poor, so they took a chance, signed to a label and got dropped a year later."[26]

The Recording Industry Structure

The music recording industry is not like other businesses. Major labels lose money on nine out of ten records, meaning they have a 90 percent failure rate. With one hit record, they must cover the costs for running the rest of their business. As a result, record label executives invest a lot of money into bands that they think might succeed, but if success is not forthcoming, the label is likely to temper its support or drop the band altogether. A lot of bands are also told that when they sign a record deal, they will retain some artistic control. The reality, however, is that the record label will ultimately determine what single will be released, if it releases any at all. When such string pulling occurs, many bands feel that the record labels are responsible for the demise of their careers. But Perry Watts-Russell, an artist-and-repertoire representative for Capitol Records in the mid-1990s, believes that the record industry is like any other business and that artists should be aware of their place in that business:

> It's a fool's game to spend your life blaming the record company. Every label can break a band, every label can't. Ultimately it's in the band's hands. So anybody who thinks "Oh, now we have a major deal, we're home, we're safe, we're gonna succeed [is

Bands like Alice in Chains helped usher Seattle's grunge rock sound onto mainstream radio airwaves.

wrong]. . . . Record companies screw up possibly everything they can screw up. . . . It's part of the nature of all corporate organizations.[27]

The Dandy Warhols, a band that signed with Capitol Records in 1996, disagrees with the way major labels handle their artists. Lead singer Courtney Taylor believes that the reason indie music reestablished itself in the late 1990s was because more and more bands had negative experiences—such as lack of promotion—with the major labels. For example, although Capitol spent four hundred thousand dollars on a music video for the Dandy Warhols shortly after signing the band, company executives quickly changed their minds about promoting the band and never released the video. The band was mostly ignored by its label, but because it had signed a contract it could not look to another label to help promote its music. Taylor says, "Indie rock happened because of this, you know, because of what we have experienced being on a major label, what every major label says won't happen to you. They won't tell you what single to put out, they won't take your pop song. That's just bad advertising for the band. . . . If I'd only been just a little bit smarter."[28]

Back to the Underground
Once grunge music had entered into the mainstream, many musicians and labels retreated to the underground as a way of protesting the major-label music structure and the supposed selling out of alternative music. Some believed that to remain truly independent they had to avoid the mainstream music industry entirely. The lead singer of Beat Happening, Calvin Johnson, went on to form indie label K Records with Candace Pederson. Other labels with similar agendas formed in resistance to the typical grunge sound, including Kill Rock Stars. Lead singer and guitarist Mac McCaughan of popular college-rock band Superchunk was courted by major labels but refused to sign with them. Instead he and fellow bandmate Laura Balance formed Merge Records, which would remain one of the more well-known and successful independent labels. Merge was modeled on the sense that even selling a few thousand records could earn both the band and the label some money.

Many independent labels were able to offer bands a much greater chance at success on their own terms. A band might not become rich,

The Brian Jonestown Massacre has made several records and toured without the aid of major-label dollars.

but it might be able to sell a few thousand records and keep a much larger portion of the profits than if the band was signed to a major label. Corey Rusk, the founder of independent label Touch & Go, operated his business on the honor system, using verbal agreements instead of complexly written contracts muddled with legal writing. Rusk has always paid bands 50 percent of the net profits of their records, which is four times the standard royalty rate in the corporate music industry. Although the label did not offer huge advances like the major labels, the profit-split system was in

some cases better financially for bands. For example, an album that sells fifty thousand records might earn a band more money in the long run than if it had signed up for a large advance and a smaller percent of net sales. In return for the profit-split, Touch & Go had the right to press the records as the market demanded them.

Some bands went to extremes to remain independent and outside of the record industry. The Brian Jonestown Massacre, a band that was playing what some critics called a postmodern 1960s revivalist music, was a band that adamantly believed that to stay

Fighting Back

The first indie music was partly a rebellion against the way major record labels conducted business. In recent years, even bands and artists that have found success on major labels have started speaking out against the record industry. Courtney Love, lead singer of the popular 1990s alternative rock act Hole, describes why she believes record companies take advantage of artists in their business practices.

R ecord companies have a 3% success rate. That means that 3% of all records released by major labels go gold or platinum. How do record companies get away with a 97% failure rate that would be totally unacceptable in any other business? Record companies keep almost all the profits. Recording artists get paid a tiny fraction of the money earned by their music. That allows record executives to be incredibly sloppy in running their companies and still create enormous amounts of cash for the corporations that own them. The royalty rates granted in every recording contract are very low to start with and then companies charge back every conceivable cost to an artist's royalty account. Artists pay for recording costs, video production costs, tour support, radio promotion, sales and marketing costs, packaging costs and any other cost the record company can subtract from their royalties.

Quoted in *Nation*, "On the Record: Toward a Union Label," April 23, 2001, p. 32.

---

true to its artistic intentions, it had to resist the pressures of the corporate music industry. The band played small venues with sometimes just a handful of people in the audience. The band could record as much music as it wanted on the independent Bomp! label. For instance, in 1996 the band produced three full-length albums. And according to lead singer Anton Newcombe, it cost just seventeen dollars to record the album *Thank God for Mental Illness.* Newcombe once commented on the desire to sell his music for a profit: "I'm not for sale. . . . The Beatles were for sale, I give it [music] away."[29]

The Brian Jonestown Massacre was still able to gain fans by remaining independent. The band was able to make records without a major record deal, and it was able to tour. It also landed on magazine covers despite not having the backing of the corporate music industry.

There were several artists who preferred to make music this way. Some, however, would question the merits of remaining truly independent. For instance, the Brian Jonestown Massacre band members were often broke and had no real homes. Sometimes they lived with friends; other times they traded their music for a house to live in and food to eat. Many indie bands that chose to tour on their own often found themselves living in similar situations. Some bands worked regular jobs in order to make a living and played their music on the side. Carlo McCormick of *Paper*, a magazine devoted to pop culture, describes the difficulty Newcombe faced making a living as a musician while also adhering to his artistic principle of not selling out. "He thinks success and credibility are mutually exclusive terms, which is an easy bag to inherit, but a difficult one to haul through every decision of your career because as a musician you want to reach the biggest possible audience and as an artist you want to impact culture in the deepest way possible."[30]

In Search of New Music

The success of grunge forever changed the nature of how new music was heard. After grunge had run its course in the mainstream, record executives, recognizing the power of youth music, again turned to the underground music scene in search of new music. In fact, in 1996 many critics predicted another underground music explosion. There were several highly anticipated CDs put out in 1996 by Sebadoh, Guided By Voices, and Archers of Loaf. Yet mainstream radio was still dominated by grunge and hard-rock bands, and the public did not yet embrace these bands. These bands did, however, build decent-size followings on the college radio circuit. A few years later though, this underground music would emerge in the mainstream— this time it would be called indie rock.

Chapter Five

Indie Rock Explodes

Although independent rock music has been made for decades, the musical genre known as indie rock did not officially exist until the middle to late 1990s. Once grunge had gone mainstream and saturated the market, record labels and corporate executives hatched the term *indie rock* to represent the "new" alternative music market in their advertising and marketing campaigns. Although there were plenty of indie rock bands in the late 1990s, it was not until 2004 that *indie rock* became a familiar and recognizable term among the mainstream record-buying public. In November of that year, indie rock poster boy Conor Oberst claimed the two top spots on the singles charts. By 2005 Death Cab for Cutie debuted at number four on the Billboard 200 with its record *Plans*. In fact, according to music critics and those in charge of the charts, the top ten records in 2005 were all catergorized as indie rock. In that same year independent record labels claimed more than 28 percent of the music-market sales worldwide.

The success of independent record labels owes a lot to the fact that indie rock has been marketed and promoted as the next youth music. Indie rock bands can be heard in commercials and popular television shows and seen on MTV. Indie rock is everywhere. Furthermore, there are countless subgenres of music that all fall under the indie rock umbrella, bringing even more attention to the scene. Indie music festivals are touted around the country as the place to hear the newest music. Being "indie" is not adhering to a specific style of music; instead, it is embracing the spirit, integrity, and youthful energy of making a music that supposedly tries hard not to compromise artistic goals for corporate sponsorship.

The popularity of indie rock and indie labels is reshaping the recording industry. Major labels are recognizing the benefits of operating their labels more like independent ones. Some big labels are buying out indie labels but keeping the business structure intact to continue the successful model. Other major labels are creating divisions within themselves that operate like indies. As a result, the boundary between what constitutes independent music and corporate music is indistinct. No longer do independent labels and major labels seem to be on opposing teams. While some artists and labels in the movement retain a do-it-yourself (DIY) ethic and independent spirit, that mentality means something different than it did in the days of early punk and hardcore. Many critics wonder if the indie rock scene will fade out like grunge or whether it will survive far into the twenty-first century.

A Return to DIY

The popularity of indie rock has had a lot to do with advances in technology that have allowed greater numbers of

In November 2004, Conor Oberst (pictured) claimed the top two spots on the Billboard Hot 100 singles chart.

artists to produce music on an independent label. So, at the same time that the genre is being orchestrated, in part by major labels, there is also some sense of DIY that remains. In the early 1990s, when CDs were becoming increasingly popular, they were expensive to produce if a band was interested in pressing less than five thousand CDs. The setup costs and minimum-run requirements kept a lot of bands from making their own CDs. By the mid-1990s, however, many more independent manufacturers were available to bands. Some of these smaller manufacturers would do runs of less than one thousand CDs and charge roughly a dollar per unit. Some bands even shared the costs by creating split CDs with other bands.

There were also several independent recording studios available to musicians. Record producer Steve Albini built his own recording studio to serve independent musicians. He worked on a sliding payment scale and sometimes offered bands his services for free. He also worked to demystify the process of making CDs. On one band's CD that he produced, the sleeve stated, "This was not mastered directly to metal or pressed into 165 grams of virgin dye-blackened vinyl. There is, in fact, nothing at all special about the manufacture of this compact disc."[31]

As technology became more sophisticated, more bands began to record themselves in home studios. With a computer and a CD burner, any band could record its music onto a CD. Many bands then passed out their homemade CDs at shows. This became standard practice for any band starting out, and it allowed the band complete control over the distribution of its music.

Emo: A Real Sound?

Another reason that indie rock has been so far-reaching is that the genre encompasses a wide array of subgenres, or offshoots. Many of these subgenres started in small scenes much like indie rock did. And much like indie rock, they have been marketed to indie rock audiences as being a very specialized music. Some of these newer categories include postrock, ambient, slow core, space rock, improv noise, theory punk, math rock, and emo.

One of the offshoots of indie rock that garnered a lot of attention in the 1990s and early twenty-first century—and has contributed to the overall popularity of indie rock—is emo. As they did with the term *indie rock*, many record companies appropriated the term *emo* as a marketing tool to sell albums. *Emo* is short for "emotional music." Emo, like indie rock, is difficult to define. This is due to the fact that musicians often do not want to be labeled emo because it locks them into a particular category of music—one that is often dismissed by a lot musicians and critics as overly weepy and self-indulgent. Author Jim DeRogatis disagrees with that description: "I prefer to think of it as punk rock that's

The Difficulty of Remaining Independent

Some bands and labels maintain the idea that to be truly independent, they must avoid all relationships with the major record industry. Greg Werckman, the general manager of Alternative Tentacles, an independent record label based in San Francisco, comments on the difficulty of remaining purely independent, using distributor Caroline Records as an example.

Alternative Tentacles is distributed exclusively through Mordam Records. Mordam in turn sells to other stores and distributors including Caroline. Granted, in a perfect world we wouldn't want to have anything to do with distributors like Caroline and Relativity. But if we can use their channels to spread our message around and hopefully enlighten some people, I don't think it's a legitimate problem. The people at Caroline that I've met are pretty cool and seem to really enjoy the music and our ideals. Unfortunately, in just about all aspects of our life, one can trace back to a major corporation. A percent of every CD is paid to the Philips Corporation because they have the copyright on the format. Does this mean everyone that makes CDs is bad and part of the evil arms building empire? If I drink coke, wear Nike shoes, drive a Volvo or any foreign car or use gasoline in my car, should I [be] chastised? Is it worse to support arms building or destroy the environment by wasting paper or driving my car? This politically correct stuff is usually too dogmatic and, believe me, fighting with people that use Caroline to distribute independent records is fighting your own team. Know your enemy. Plus once again, where is the punk rule book and does everyone have to play by it?

Quoted in Brian Zero, "Corporate Rock, Punk?" *Maximum RocknRoll*, June 1994. www.arancidamoeba.com/mrr.corporaterock.html.

more melodic and introspective/depressing than hardcore, but still tapping into that primal energy and anger."[32]

Indie Music Festivals

One of the trends that helped popularize the indie rock genre—and its many subgenres—was the regular exhibition of bands in packaged music festivals. There are several American festivals that take place each year to showcase indie bands. Some of the most recognizable are North by Northwest in Portland, Oregon; South by Southwest in Austin, Texas; and the College Media Journal (CMJ) Music Marathon in New York City. The CMJ festival was originally created in 1980 to help bring together college radio stations from around the country. It was an important avenue for independent record labels to get exposure and for college radio stations to discover new music.

In the fall of 2005, more than one thousand bands converged on New York City to play the weeklong CMJ festival. Well-established indie rock acts like the New Pornographers, who occupied the top spot on CMJ's college-radio chart, played sold-out shows. At the 2004 festival the unknown Canadian indie rock band the Arcade Fire gained exposure after playing several small shows during the festival. Shortly after appearing at the festival, it released its critically acclaimed album *Funeral* on the indie label Merge. The exposure at the festival created a small fan base that

bought the album. The band gained a large following in a short amount of time, partly due to word of mouth and partly due to radio airplay. The band headlined the festival the following year.

Though the larger indie festivals were initially started to feature independent musicians, over the years they have become so popular that critics fear the events are no longer about connecting new bands with interested audiences. For instance, the CMJ festival is now regularly attended by increasing numbers of label scouts looking for potential bands to sign. Similarly, South by Southwest has become what some observers consider a spring break destination catering to a party crowd and not appreciative fans. Some of the larger festivals also show signs of corporate influences because advertising has become a key component in the success of the festival. Many festivals are also intermixing musical venues with panels, display booths, and keynote speakers. The number of artists and the various added attractions only serve to raise the admission costs. For instance, a CMJ pass can exceed $445, and this price does not even guarantee admission to all of the musical performances.

As alternatives to the larger indie festivals, local festivals are cropping up in cities across America. Many of the people promoting these festivals are interested in providing lesser-known and local bands an opportunity to play in a festival environment. San

Neko Case of the New Pornographers performs onstage during a large indie rock festival in 2006.

Emotional Music

Like indie rock, itself, the subgenres of indie rock are just as difficult to define. Author Andy Greenwald attempts to define emo in his book Nothing Feels Good: Punk Rock, Teenagers, and Emo:

Emo isn't a genre—it's far too messy and contentious for that. What the term does signify is a particular relationship between a fan and a band. It's the desire to turn a monologue into a dialogue, to be a part of the art that affects you and to connect to it on every possible level—sentiments particularly relevant in an increasingly corporate, suburban, and diffuse culture such as ours. Emo is a specific sort of teenage longing, a romantic and ultimately self-centered need to understand the bigness of the world in relation to *you*. It takes its cues from the world-changing slap of community-oriented punk, the heart-swollen pomp of power ballads, and the gee-whiz nostalgia of guitar pop. Emo is as specific as adolescence and lasts about as long.

Andy Greenwald, *Nothing Feels Good: Punk Rock, Teenagers, and Emo.* New York: St. Martin's Griffin, 2003, p. 5.

Francisco is one city that has embraced an annual indie music festival called Noise Pop. The festival lasts for several days and features several different music venues. The aim of Noise Pop is to offer intimate settings for music lovers to see bands inexpensively. In addition, it allows independent bands to hear their peers play. Festival founder Kevin Arnold works hard to keep the festival from becoming a "record label schmooze fest." Arnold states, "They have to realize that I am not booking tons of shows of unsigned bands. That's not the point. The objective is to help everybody. Mostly just to provide bands and audiences with good cohesive shows, to make an event that raises people's eyebrows a bit."[33]

Advertising Lends National Exposure to Indie Rock

Festival promoters are not the only companies trying to profit from indie rock. Advertisers have begun to tap the indie market to find songs to use in commercials and their advertising campaigns. Advertisers use indie rock to make their products seem hip while also giving bands national exposure. For example, the Australian band Jet gained notoriety and fame after its song "Are You Gonna Be My Girl" appeared in the marketing campaigns of Apple's iPod and Vodaphone. The song also appeared on the soundtrack for the popular video game *Madden NFL 2004*.

Many artists have been approached to sell their songs for a rather hefty sum of money. In many cases, the money would double or triple the band's yearly income. Sometimes bands accept such lucrative offers in hopes of gaining national exposure, but in other cases, bands have refused to sell their indie credentials.

Indie rock bands the Thermals, Trans Am, and LiLiPUT all refused offers to have one of their songs featured in a Hummer automobile commercial. These and other bands have rejected fifty-thousand-dollar offers from the automaker due to personal principles. Most of the resistance comes from band members' concerns for the environment. Hummers have poor gas mileage, and at a time when America faces increased dependency on oil, many indie musicians do not want their names attached to a product that does not match their personal, political, and environmental views.

Many large companies are turning to indie rock to sell products because they believe the popular style of music

Commercials and advertising campaigns have helped bands like Jet (pictured) to quickly gain fame.

can help them tap younger, moneyed buyers. Lance Jensen, the president of an advertising agency representing Hummer, says he and the automaker are not trying to exploit indie music but rather see it as an opportunity to expose new artists. "We just pick music that we like as people. Being a music lover, there's so much interesting work out there, I wonder—why not let people hear it? I don't know, I guess I just want artists to make money. I don't want them to be poor."[34]

The Growth of Indie Labels

Despite having the major record industry signing bands that got their start on independent labels, indie labels are thriving. They make up an increasingly larger portion of the music market. With new technology and distribution channels opening up the music industry, independent labels are experiencing a dramatic increase in profits—sometimes as much as 50 to 100 percent each year. For instance, New West Records, formed in 1998 in Austin, Texas, doubled its business each year during the 2000 to 2002 period. Many indie labels are achieving this growth by branching out and signing bands that are playing any number of indie rock offshoots, from country rock bands to indie folk artists.

Another reason indie labels are able to succeed during a time when album sales as a whole are down is the fact that their artists' songs will not be heard on commercial radio. Large labels pay radio stations up to five hundred thousand dollars to have songs from their artists played on national radio. Indie labels are unable to afford to pay promoters that much money to get a song on the air. Thus, they are able to save a lot of money by avoiding commercial radio costs. At a major label, artists are unlikely to make a profit unless they sell at least 1 million albums. In many cases artists might only earn one dollar per CD sold, which does not add up to much after expenses like studio time and limo rides are subtracted from those costs. In contrast, indie artists might make five dollars per CD, and if they sell five thousand CDs, they earn twenty-five thousand dollars, which can help supplement their incomes.

This sort of business sense attracts increasingly large numbers to the indie music scene. Many indie labels are able to keep overhead costs down by curbing marketing and using some of the free technology and other platforms available on the Internet. Indie labels also work on building relationships with college and public radio stations as well as local retailers, which are often more interested in alternative music.

Another reason indie labels are experiencing growth is that many of them pick up albums that have already been recorded by the artists themselves. In this way, the labels can sometimes avoid recording costs.

Following Suit

Major labels are recognizing the success of indie labels as they begin to control a larger percent of the market share. Many independent labels have

A Return to College

Indie rock initially was the alternative music of college kids in the late 1990s. After the grunge scene began to fade, music shifted away from the pounding drums, grinding electric guitars, and screaming vocals of grunge music. Bands began to incorporate qualities that had been prominent in more tame college rock music. The music became more literate and included headier topics. There was an emphasis on thought-provoking and introspective song lyrics. For instance, the lyrics of indie rock band Bright Eyes focus on topics like the meaningless nature of existence and death. Wilco lead singer Jeff Tweedy's lyrics explore the various psychological states of the human mind. With the more pensive lyrics came more melodic song structures that fit the mood better than distorted guitar riffs.

been bought by major record companies. Other independent labels are partially owned by one of the majors. Sometimes fans are not even aware that a label that once was independent might have become an affiliate of a major. These buyouts and mergers have created complex relationships between artists, labels, and distribution companies (which are used by both indie companies and major labels).

There are many successful indie labels that have refused to succumb to major-label influence, however. Saddle Creek, a successful indie label located in Omaha, Nebraska, is one of the leading indie labels and has refused several buyout offers from major labels. Saddle Creek cofounder Robb Nansel talks about the label's decision to remain independent:

> For me it's always been, "Let's see how far we can take it on our own." I always thought there was no way we could sell 100,000 records. I think I looked up *The Lonesome Crowded West*, that Modest Mouse record, and that's what they sold, so that seemed like the indie peak. But *Lifted* [Bright Eyes' 2002 debut album] sold 250,000. So [we will remain independent] as long as we can continue to move forward and not feel like we're hurting the record with things we can't do.[35]

In other cases, major labels have begun to adjust their business practices to resemble the structure of independent labels. To do so, they have had to adopt some typically indie characteristics, like giving the artists more control over the kind of music they produce. This can be both a positive and a negative for bands recording music. For instance, after recording their fourth album, *Yankee Hotel Foxtrot*, Wilco's record label, Reprise, decided not to release it because the label thought it was too experimental and would alienate fans. The executives at Reprise feared that sales would be too low and demanded the band make the album more "listener friendly." Wilco, however, chose not to change the music just to make it commercially viable. Instead, the band bought back the album rights for fifty thousand dollars and left the label. Lead singer Jeff

Tweedy comments on the band's unwillingness to compromise: "The only negative was that it hurt for a couple of days that someone hated my record so much. We got over it really fast. And then we were just people who play music together. We didn't have a record deal, we weren't touring, we weren't selling anything, and it felt better than ever to be in a rock band."[36]

Shortly after leaving Reprise, the band posted the album on its Web site, streaming the songs for free. The album received positive reviews from fans and critics, and it was not long before another label picked up the album. Ironically, it was Reprise's sister label—Nonesuch—which falls under the Warner Music Group, that signed

In some cases, indie rock artists will make more money per each CD sold than do their mainstream counterparts.

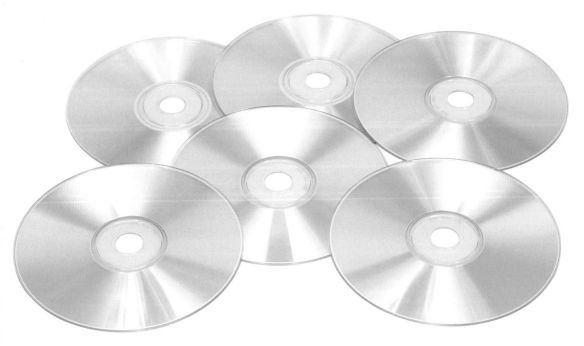

Noise Pop

Noise Pop began in 1993 and was organized by local San Franciscan Kevin Arnold, a Berkeley grad and band-booking agent. In order to fill a dead January night at a venue called the Kennel Club, Arnold decided to put together a small showcase of five underground indie acts. To promote the night, he hung home-made posters around town with the catchy phrase *Noise Pop*. More than eight hundred people attended the showcase that night. Arnold was encouraged to make it a yearly event in the hopes of filling what appeared to be a void in the local music scene. Each year the festival gained more attention, and by the third year of the festival, Arnold had booked 28 groups to play over a period of four days. The festival is still going strong after more than a decade, and in 2006 the Noise Pop festival featured close to 150 bands over the course of seven days. As the festival grows each year, there is more interest by the mainstream music industry. Several indie bands that have headlined Noise Pop, including the White Stripes, Jimmy Eat World, and Modest Mouse, have gone on to earn critical acclaim and mainstream radio airplay.

Frontman Isaac Brock of Modest Mouse plays a banjo at an indie rock festival.

the band. In Wilco's case, it worked in the band's favor to take a chance and make the album without buckling to major-label pressures. The band's uncompromising ideals and artistic integrity make it something of a legend in the indie rock world despite being signed by an affiliate of a major.

Some fans and critics worry that the more that independent labels and major labels resemble each other, the less likely truly independent music will be heard. Writer Ryan Gillespie wonders, "So in a world where the mainstream sounds like the underground and the underground acts like the mainstream, what happens to truly underground music? When major labels buy indie bands by the cart and the indie labels act and operate like major labels, how does a truly independent release get heard?"[37]

A Bright Future

Despite not having a concrete past or a definitive future, the indie rock genre remains one of the most popular styles of music today. Increasing numbers of indie rock artists are making and recording albums—and not just on independent labels. It seems that if a band has put in years of hard work on an indie label and maintains an image of independence, it is more acceptable for the band to sign with a major label. The genre itself has become looser in terms of what is considered indie rock. As a result, the future of indie rock looks limitless as indie rock bands and indie labels are adopting and using the technological advances that are affecting the music industry as a whole. Indie rock is at the forefront of shaping the future of the music industry in the twenty-first century.

Chapter Six

The Future of Indie Rock

In 2006 the fastest-selling debut album in U.K. chart history came from the English indie rock band Arctic Monkeys. The band's first album, titled *Whatever People Say I Am, That's What I'm Not*, was released in January and sold more than 360,000 copies in less than a week. Within that first week, the band's album sold more copies than the rest of those on the Top 20 album chart combined. What is unique about the band is that it did not make it to the top as a result of a record label's marketing campaign but instead built up its fan base entirely from the Internet. The demo CDs the band handed out at shows in 2003 were posted and circulated on the Web—not by band members but by their fans. In 2005, with the band's album as yet unreleased, its debut single hit number one on the U.K. music charts, followed by its second single. The band eventually signed with independent record label Domino Records. According to a music retailer for the British chain HMV, "In terms of sheer impact . . . we haven't seen anything quite like this since The Beatles. In the space of just a few weeks the Arctic Monkeys have gone from being relative newcomers to becoming a household name."[38]

The Arctic Monkeys are only one of the many independent bands that are achieving success as a result of the Internet. The many Web-based tools available on the Internet are leveling the playing field for indie rock musicians. Digital music Web sites and online streaming are just two of the tools that are helping bands promote and distribute their music to a much broader audience. The Web has democratized the music industry, replacing traditional modes of distribution and promotion (which were mainly controlled by large record companies) with new technologies that are accessible to the masses. The Internet is especially appealing to those artists and musicians who are hoping to attract new listeners to their music.

Artists from all musical genres are engaging the new technology, but indie rockers are especially drawn to it because it fits well with the do-it-yourself (DIY) ethic of their predecessors. And sharing music via the Internet has spawned a whole new generation of truly independent musicians who can record their own music, burn their own CDs, and distribute their own music, all without the help of any label at all. The development of Web-based tools bodes well for many indie rock artists in the future. It seems to be invigorating the idea of independence that seemed to have been going by the wayside with the popularity of the indie rock genre. It is unclear whether the genre of indie rock will still refer to music made on independent labels or whether it will become something entirely new.

Opportunities to Sample New Music

In the past, indie rock bands and musicians used touring, word of mouth, fan clubs, and posters to promote their music. Many bands relied on traditional industry channels like radio and

The Arctic Monkeys (pictured) are one of many indie rock bands that rapidly gained notice through the Internet.

MTV to gain recognition. Today there are several grassroots Web tools that provide new opportunities for independent musicians to share their music with a wider fan base. Web sites, blogs, listener recommendations, online music samples, and shared playlists are many of the new elements of the online world that are impacting indie rock music in the twenty-first century. These tools allow a greater number of independent artists to be heard while at the same time allowing consumers greater choice in their musical selection.

There are several Web sites that operate virtual storefronts in order to sell music online. For the past several years iTunes has been the most popular site to purchase music. Most songs on iTunes cost 99¢, and albums can be purchased typically for a price between $9.99 and $12.99. There is less risk to consumers in buying music by the song because if the purchasers do not like what they hear, they might only be out a dollar, versus the $10 to $18 they might have lost if they had bought an entire CD. With such an easy way to purchase music, people are willing to buy new music that might not be carried in their local record stores or played on commercial radio. For example, iTunes has as many as seven hundred thousand songs available in its online music library.

In addition to purchasing music on the Internet, there are several online music subscription services, including Napster, Yahoo, and RealNetworks' Rhapsody, that allow patrons to download from their select music libraries. Some sites allow listeners to hear snippets of songs, and others allow unlimited music downloads for a monthly fee. Fans enjoy such sites because it is much easier to experiment with new music by sampling one or two songs from a band. However, the recording industry claims that cheaper downloads translate into fewer CDs being sold. The industry has been fighting these advances because it feels it is losing revenue as a result of Internet music sales and unrestricted file sharing among users.

Radio Indie Rock

Internet radio is another Web-based tool that is helping indie rock bands reach new markets and connect with audiences around the world. Bands previously relied on the FM radio market or local college radio stations to play their songs. The Internet, however, has changed all of that in recent years. No longer do music fans rely on commercial radio to hear new music. Hundreds of independent radio stations have popped up on the Internet to offer alternatives to mainstream music. For instance, Radio Indie Rock, an Internet radio station dedicated to playing indie music, launched in June 2003.

Unlike traditional college radio, where broadcasting is confined to small areas (unless the show happens to be syndicated), Internet radio is not limited by narrow bandwidths or frequencies. Obscure radio shows playing even more obscure music can be accessed by anyone with a computer. A listener in Australia can log onto Internet radio stations streaming music from Canada, the United States, or Great Britain. As a result, Internet radio offers indie rock bands greater opportunities to promote and distribute their music to a worldwide audience.

Internet radio shows are becoming increasingly popular, and like college radio, labels are looking to these programs to discover new bands. Some of the more successful Internet radio programs have been noticed by the music industry. In some cases, the top Internet songs end up on the charts of industry magazines such as *Radio & Records* and *CMJ*.

Although the Internet has provided lots of growth for indie rock bands, it has not eliminated the traditional college radio format. In 2006 there were 453 college radio stations in the United States. As a result, many indie rock bands are continuing to find audiences on college radio. For instance, Sleater-Kinney, Stephen Malkmus, Bright Eyes, the Decemberists, the New Pornographers, Tortoise, and Sufjan Stevens were all able to support midsize tours due to their exposure on college radio.

Web Sites and Webzines: The Fanzines of the Future

Music stores, subscription services, and Internet radio are just a few of the ways technology has provided indie rock with greater exposure. Like their fanzine predecessors, many Web sites have created "Webzines" to introduce lesser-known or experimental music to listeners around the world. These Web sites create a community for independent-minded fans in the music industry. Many of these sites provide links to bands'

Modern computers offer several tools that provide new opportunities for indie musicians to discover larger fan bases.

The Future of Music Coalition

The Future of Music Coalition (FMC) began in 2000 to explore how advances in technology, such as online music trading, was changing the way music was recorded and distributed. The nonprofit organization includes members who are part of the music, technology, and public-policy communities. Their goal is to educate the public, the media, and policy makers about the issues relating to music and technology. The organization wants individuals —both artists and other creators— to benefit from the new technology, with the hope of decreasing the power of major labels, major media, and chain-store monopolies.

One of the major issues is that the revenue that artists receive from radio play and the sale of records decreases with the use of peer-to-peer trading with services like Napster and KaZaa. The public can more easily enjoy music not controlled by the mainstream channels, but artists are put in compromising positions. If they support the current music industry and argue against such services, they are often considered greedy. However, if they support such services, then they experience a loss of income. The FMC is working to find new models of music distribution that benefit both the independent artists and the public.

Web sites, electronic magazines, independent music news, and music samples of featured bands. The goal of many of these Web sites is to expose people to bands they would not see on television or read about in major publications.

For instance, Brainwashed.com is a Web site that was established in 1997 as a way to provide fans with firsthand information about new music. Started by devoted music fan Jon Whitney, Brainwashed.com features more than fifty bands on its site, including the bands Matmos and Tortoise. Brainwashed.com offers a weekly Webzine, the *Brain*, which features music articles, album reviews, and music samples. The site is more than just a promotion opportunity for bands, however. It has become a music community that connects people from around the world.

Many of these independent Web sites have the ability to launch the careers of relatively unknown bands. For example, in early 2005 the New York indie rock band Clap Your Hands Say Yeah was unsigned and unknown. Without a label, band members had been pressing CDs themselves and selling them at concerts and via the Internet. However, the band came to the attention of Dan Beirne, who discovered the group's music while visiting a file-sharing Web site. He posted a review of the band on Stereogum.com, a popular Web site hosting blogs about music. Soon other blogs were written about the band; by June, Pitchforkmedia. com, the premier site devoted to indie music, had reviewed a track from the band. A year later Clap Your Hands Say Yeah had sold fifty thousand CDs and had one of its songs played on the NBC sitcom *The Office.*

MySpace: The New DIY

The Internet has become a seemingly limitless resource for indie rock musicians looking for new ways to promote their music. Many bands are turning to any one of the Web's many social networking sites, including Friendster, Pure Volume, TagWorld, and MySpace, as an alternative to traditional promotion methods. These sites allow indie rock newcomers to share their music with a large audience—without having to be signed to any music label at all. However, many well-established indie acts are also recognizing the power of these social networking sites to reach audiences. For instance, several popular indie rock groups have joined TagWorld, including Death Cab for Cutie, the Postal Service, and the Shins. Many of these bands are composed of young people who are tapped into the technological world and recognize the Internet as a forum to further connect with audiences.

By far the most popular of the social networking sites is MySpace.com. With roughly 43 million members, MySpace has become the third-most-visited Web domain on the Internet. Though the site was originally created for people to meet other people, in 2004 musical artists were allowed to design band profiles on the site as well as stream MP3s of their songs. Some bands even allowed their music to be downloaded free of charge. Eventually bands began to use MySpace to promote albums, announce shows, upload songs and videos, as well as interact with fans. In early 2005 some three hundred thousand bands were profiled on the MySpace network; by 2006 that number had doubled to six hundred thousand. Tom Anderson, a cofounder and president of MySpace, describes the appeal of the site: "Bands are going to MySpace because it's free and they don't have to know how to do a Web site. But the biggest reason is because there are 43 million people on MySpace."[39]

MySpace has decreased the amount of time and money bands spend on

The New York-based indie band Clap Your Hands Say Yeah pressed and sold its own CDs before getting discovered via the Internet.

development and promotion. In the past, bands could spend hours putting up concert posters around town and sending CDs to radio stations. With MySpace, concert and news information about a band can be spread through the MySpace community in a matter of seconds. The Brooklyn, New York, indie rock band Coppermine has a profile on MySpace. The band's page has drawn nearly three hundred thousand visitors, and it has been added as a "friend" to more than one hundred and fifteen thousand users. As a result of Coppermine's presence on MySpace, the band has been contacted by managers, promoters, Webzines, and music labels.

Jonathan Buck, the lead singer and guitarist for the band, comments on MySpace as a promotional tool: "A MySpace profile is so efficient and so effective that it supplants a lot of that other stuff [radio play, magazine write-ups, and street teams]."[40]

Even major recording labels are turning to MySpace to help promote upcoming releases because it is an inexpensive way to reach a large audience. For example, Interscope featured Queens of the Stone Age, Beck, and Nine Inch Nails on MySpace prior to the release of their albums. Interscope even allowed MySpace users to preview songs from the albums. According to MySpace chief executive officer

MySpace cofounders Tom Anderson (right) and Chris DeWolfe have offered indie bands the chance to design band profiles online and stream MP3s for free.

Chris DeWolfe, "Labels understand people are spending more time online than on other mediums. Radio is more constrained. MTV is down to about 10 videos a day. MySpace has become the place for awareness of new music and exclusive content. We can point music out ahead of its official release in a very organic way."[41]

Like other new technology, networking sites like MySpace and Tag-World offer bands new ways of thinking about music distribution.

New Distribution Channels Emerge

Traditionally, independent rockers have struggled to get their music distributed. Many bands might be able to save up enough money to record their music, but it was not always easy to find a label or distributor that would promote the music to record stores or even to mail-order catalogs. Manufacturing and distribution monopolies give five labels control over 90 percent of all music sold. This means that 90 percent of artists have to get a deal with one of the major record labels—or one of their subsidiaries—in order to have their albums sold in the marketplace. This gives independent musicians and labels only 10 percent of the distribution outlets.

Due to recent advances in technology on the Internet, however, indie labels are finding themselves better equipped to adapt to the changing music industry. By 2003 indie music labels accounted for $8 billion, or 25 percent of the $32 billion global music market. As more and more bands become familiar with the Internet as a source for distributing music, it is likely that the indie market share will continue to grow.

The increased indie presence is a direct result of companies that serve as liaisons between music labels and the online music services. Companies such as Digital Rights Agency and Independent Online Distribution Alliance help small labels negotiate inclusion of indie music within the online music stores. These agencies even negotiate royalty rates. Tuhin Roy, the founder of the Digital Rights Agency, acknowledges the difficulty of bargaining for competitive rates for indie rock bands. "It's still a struggle in most cases to get rates that are competitive with the majors. It's only through the collective bargaining power of organizations like ours that we're getting close."[42]

CD Baby and Loudeye are two other Web companies that help artists without a label find music services to distribute their music. CD Baby is the largest seller of independent CDs on the Web and has been helping unsigned bands sell their music online since 1997. It hosts an online retail store where any band can sell its CDs. The service also helps artists sell their music on digital retail spaces like iTunes, Rhapsody, and Emusic. CD Baby only sells CDs that come directly from musicians, which allows the musicians to earn a much greater percentage of the CD sale. For instance, in most distribution deals artists might only make one to two dollars per CD, but with CD Baby artists can make anywhere from six to twelve dollars per CD.

Since its start, CD Baby has sold close to 2.5 million CDs and represents close to 131,000 artists. Alex Steininger of CD Baby reinforces the notion that CD Baby was designed to help artists distribute their music without a record label:

Yes, that was the goal with CD Baby, to offer an artist a way to do it themselves, to not need anyone else, and have this availability out there if there was demand. So people could find the product and purchase it, once the artist

Anyone Can Be a DJ

Internet radio stations operate much like college radio stations —disc jockeys (DJs) create personal playlists of bands that interest them, often purposefully ignoring bands that make the playlists of mainstream radio and MTV formats. The Internet format, however, allows almost anyone to become a DJ and design a personal playlist that is featured on the Web site. For instance, Radio Indie Rock hosts DJs from New York to San Francisco to Toronto and Ottawa, Canada. One indie rock station, Live365, located at www.live365. com, encourages independent DJs to design and run their own Webcasts. Recording and uploading a show requires minimal equipment: two CD players, one microphone, a computer, audio recording software, and a large music collection.

The band Everclear performs live during a Webcast concert.

Is the Internet a Threat?

Whereas many indie musicians and their fans are thrilled with the seemingly endless opportunities to disseminate new music via the Internet, the record industry is not. When music is traded via file sharing (when users are able to access other users music libraries) or is downloaded for free, the record industry loses out on the opportunity to make money on the sale of that music. Fearing the loss of revenue, the record industry has filed a number of lawsuits arguing copyright infringements because the sites in most cases have not been given permission to copy the music. Many record labels claim that CD sales are down, which has resulted in a loss of revenue. Although some artists support the record industry's attempt to control music traded on the Internet, others feel that the lawsuits hurt those very people whom the record industry is claiming to protect. Jon Whitney, the founder of Brainwashed.com, an independent music Web site, feels the recording industry's argument is weak:

The RIAA [Recording Industry Association of America] is a beast just fighting to stay alive. The genie is out of the bottle already and there's nothing they can stop about it. About 25 years ago they were all up in arms again about the dual-recording tape decks. They thought this would kill music, but it didn't. When they file lawsuits and launch large campaigns, they're hurting so many people. It's expensive and it takes away money from the artists and to support bands and tours. I don't know any record label employee who makes a living wage or any major label artist with health benefits. However, the fat lawyers and RIAA execs seem to pocket a bundle.

Quoted in Suzanne Bestler, "Persistence Is All: A Conversation with Jon Whitney of Brainwashed. com," *Afterimage*, January/February 2004, p. 16.

created the demand. And as we grow, we find new ways to help independent artists. Helping artists has, and always will be, our end mission with CD Baby.[43]

Will Indie Rock Last?

As advances in music making and communications technology continue, the future of indie rock music seems limitless. Despite this, *indie rock* remains a fluid or even questionable term. Although the Internet offers new ways of distributing music, the sound of indie rock remains as varied as it has always been. Certainly many bands that release some sort of rock-sounding music on the Internet could fall into the indie rock category since their music has not been recorded on one of the major labels. However, does *indie rock* still only refer to music recorded on independent labels? What about the bands that self-produce and self-record? What of the thousands of bands that release one or two songs via the Internet? With seemingly unlimited access to bands on the Internet and the demystifying of the music industry, perhaps what might be termed *indie rock* today will simply become the standard way of making music in the future.

Indie rock continues to raise many unanswered questions about what it is. One thing is certain: it seems to be the latest phase in the cyclical nature of youth-oriented rock-and-roll music. Perhaps the term *indie rock* will become obsolete as it is replaced by the next catchy phrase co-opted by those interested in tapping into a new market. Perhaps indie rock will eventually solidify itself into a definable term. Or perhaps it will further splinter into endless subgenres as the Internet and technological advances change the very nature of how music is produced and recorded. Despite the difficulty in understanding what indie rock is, the creation and distribution of music independent of major-label support is a thriving industry in its own right. More independently produced music is reaching more listeners today than ever before. *Indie rock* could be the name for that music, or it could be the entire revolution that is reconfiguring the record industry and giving myriad new artists the chance to be heard.

• Notes •

Introduction: What Is Indie Rock?

1. Ryan Hibbett, "What Is Indie Rock" *Popular Music and Society*, 2005. www.findarticles.com/p/articles/mi _m2822/is_1_28/ai_n9507897.

Chapter One: Punk: The Angry Scream of Disaffected Youth

2. Greil Marcus, *In the Fascist Bathroom: Punk in Pop Music, 1977–1992*. Cambridge, MA: Harvard University Press, 1993, p. 2.

3. Hibbett, "What Is Indie Rock?"

4. Quoted in A.S. Van Dorston, "What Are the Politics of Boredom?" *Fast 'n' Bulbous* music webzine. www. fastnbulbous.com/punk.htm.

5. Quoted in Van Dorston, "What Are the Politics of Boredom?"

6. Quoted in Van Dorston, "What Are the Politics of Boredom?"

7. Quoted in James Gregory, "Interview: Buzzcocks," PitchFork Media, February 20, 2006. www.pitch forkmedia.com/interviews/b/buzz cocks-06.

8. Quoted in Steven Wells, *Punk: Young, Loud & Snotty*. New York: Thunder's Mouth, 2004, p. 7.

9. Quoted in Gregory, "Interview: Buzzcocks."

Chapter Two: A Do-It-Yourself Mentality

10. Quoted in Bob Stanley, "The Birth of the Uncool," *Guardian* (Manchester) March 31, 2006. http:// arts.guardian.co.uk/filmand music/story/0,,1742844,00.html.

11. Quoted in Graham Lock, "Desperate Bicycles," *New Musical Express*, October 14, 1978.

12. Quoted in Paul Rosen, "'It Was Easy, It Was Cheap, Go and Do It!' Technology and Anarchy in the UK Music Industry," in *Twenty-First Century Anarchism: Unorthodox Ideas for a New Millennium*, ed. Jonathan Purkis and James Bowen. London: Cassell, 1997.

13. Michael Azzerad, *Our Band Could Be Your Life*. New York: Back Bay, 2001, p. 10.

14. Quoted in Dave Thompson, *Alternative Rock*. San Francisco: Miller Freeman, 2000, p. 52.

Chapter Three: College Rock

15. Hugo Lindgren, "I Love the Eighties," *New York*. www.newyork metro.com/nymetro/arts/music/pop /reviews/12305/index.html.

16. Quoted in Meredith Levine, "At WYBC, Old Guard and Ratings Push Clash," *Yale Herald*, March 1,

2002. www.yaleherald.com/article. php?Article=292.

17. Quoted in Levine, "At WYBC, Old Guard and Ratings Push Clash."

18. Quoted in Steve Pond, "In the Real World," *Rolling Stone*, December 3, 1987. www.rollingstone.com/news/story/5938674/in_the_real_world.

19. Quoted in Heidi Sherman, "Sebadoh Slip from Indie Shackles," *Rolling Stone*, February 22, 1999. www.rollingstone.com/news/story/5923105/sebadoh_slip_from_indieshackles.

Chapter Four: The Selling of Grunge Music

20. Quoted in Kurt St. Thomas and Troy Smith, *Nirvana: The Chosen Rejects*. New York: St. Martin's, 2004, p. 6.

21. Quoted in St. Thomas and Smith, *Nirvana*, p. 16.

22. Quoted in *Hype!*, DVD. Los Angeles: Republic Pictures, 1996.

23. Quoted in Thomas L. Bell, "Why Seattle? An Examination of an Alternative Rock Culture Hearth," *Journal of Cultural Geography*, Fall/Winter 1998.

24. Quoted in Michael Azzerad, "Grunge City: On the Seattle Scene," *Rolling Stone*, April 16, 1992, p. 44.

25. Quoted in *Hype!*

26. Quoted in Steve Gdula, "Archers of Loaf Keep DIY Attitude," *Rolling Stone*, September 18, 1998. www.rollingstone.com.

27. Quoted in *Dig!*, DVD, directed and produced by Ondi Timoner. Los Angeles, CA: Interloper Films, 2004.

28. Quoted in *Dig!*

29. Quoted in *Dig!*

30. Quoted in *Dig!*

Chapter Five: Indie Rock Explodes

31. Jim DeRogatis, "Emo: The Genre That Dare Not Speak Its Name," *Guitar World*, 1999. www.jimdero.com/OtherWritings/Other%20emo.htm.

32. Jim DeRogatis, "Emo: The Genre That Dare Not Speak Its Name."

33. Quoted in Jordan Kurland, "Snap, Crackle, and Noise Pop," *San Francisco Examiner*, February 26, 1997, p. C.

34. Quoted in Otis Hart, "Bah Hummer: Indie Rockers Reject Big Money from the King of Gas Guzzlers," Austin360.com, February 21, 2006. www.austin360.com/music/content/music/stories/2006/02/22hummer.html.

35. Quoted in Rollingstone.com, "King of Indie Rock," January 13, 2001. www.rollingstone.com/news/story/6822956/king_of_indie_rock/print.

36. Quoted in Joan Anderman, "Wilco's Jeff Tweedy Has a Restless, at Times Alienating Creativity That

Makes the Shy Songwriter an Indie-Rock Icon," Boston.com, August 6, 2004. www.boston.com.

37. Ryan Gillespie, "Bring on the Major Leagues," PopMatters, January 26, 2006. www.popmatters.com/music/features/060126-indiemusic.shtml.

Chapter Six: The Future of Indie Rock

38. Quoted in BBC News, "Arctic Monkeys Make Chart History," January 29, 2006. http://news.bbc.co.uk/1/hi/entertainment/4660394.stm.

39. Quoted in Josh Belzman, "Bands and Fans Singing a New Tune on MySpace," MSNBC.com, February 13, 2006. www.msnbc.msn.com/id/11114166.

40. Quoted in Belzman, "Bands and Fans Singing a New Tune on MySpace."

41. Quoted in Belzman, "Bands and Fans Singing a New Tune on MySpace."

42. Quoted in John Borland, "Indie Music Riding the Digital Surge," CNET News, July 21, 2004. http://news.com.com/Indie+music+riding+the+digital+surge/2100-1027_3-5238387.html.

43. Quoted in IndieHQ, "Interview with Alex Steininger of CD Baby," April 30, 2006. http://indiehq.com/2006/04/30/interview-with-alex-steininger-of-cd-baby/#more-79.

• For Further Reading •

Books

Michael Azerrad, *Our Band Could Be Your Life*. New York: Back Bay, 2001. Azerrad profiles thirteen bands from the American indie underground during the years 1981 to 1991. Azerrad only includes bands that have recorded with an independent label for the majority of their careers. A few of the bands profiled are Black Flag, Minor Threat, the Minutemen, and Mission of Burma.

Andy Greenwald, *Nothing Feels Good: Punk Rock, Teenagers, and Emo*. New York: St. Martin's Griffin, 2003. This is the first book written about the elusive genre of emo. Greenwald explores the relationship between emo and teenagers and argues that emo is more than a musical genre—it is a teenage rite of passage.

Greil Marcus, *In the Fascist Bathroom: Punk in Pop Music*. Cambridge, MA: Harvard University Press, 1993. This book includes more than seventy short articles written about punk over the course of fifteen years. Most of the articles focus on the uncompromising nature of punk rock and how it continually reappears in pop culture as a form of artistic rebellion.

Martin C. Strong, *The Great Indie Discography*. Edinburgh, Scotland: Canongate, 2003. An extensive resource, this book chronicles the careers of indie musicians, mostly British and American, all the way from the 1960s until 2003. Each entry includes a band history, complete discography, chart listing, and recommended listening tracks.

Kurt St. Thomas and Troy Smith, *Nirvana: The Chosen Rejects*. New York: St. Martin's, 2004. The authors of this book used numbers of personal interviews with Nirvana to reconstruct the band's rise from alternative obscurity to chart-topping band. The authors include stories about the songs that came to define the Nirvana sound.

Dave Thompson, *Alternative Rock*. San Francisco: Miller Freeman, 2000. This guide highlights the alternative rock bands that changed the rock scene in the 1970s, 1980s, and 1990s by breaking the rules. Thompson provides band biographies, reviews, in-depth histories, and discographies.

David Wimble, *The Indie Bible*. New York: Music Sales, 2003. Wimble's comprehensive guide provides ample resources for independent musicians who are searching for ways to market and record their music. Using an easy-to-follow format, the book lists radio shows, Web sites, and independent labels to investigate.

DVDs

Dig! Directed and produced by Ondi Timoner. Los Angeles: Interloper Films, 2004. This documentary follows the musical careers of Anton Newcombe of the Brian Jonestown Massacre and Courtney Taylor of the Dandy Warhols over the course of seven years. The bands began as friends and tour mates but eventually became rivals as Brian Jonestown Massacre remained independent and the Dandy Warhols signed with a major label. The documentary reveals the challenges and contradictions that come with taking either route in a contentious music world.

The Flaming Lips: The Fearless Freaks. Los Angeles: Shout! Factory, 2005. Filmmaker Bradley Beasley follows the band as it recounts its past and the escapades that have made it one of alternative rock music's favorite bands. The film covers the highs and lows of the band's twenty-year career.

Hype! Los Angeles: Republic Pictures, 1996. The film explores the Seattle underground scene and the hype surrounding it after alternative music broke into the mainstream in the early 1990s. The film includes concert footage and interviews with bands such as Soundgarden, Mudhoney, and the Melvins.

I Am Trying to Break Your Heart: A Film About Wilco. Directed by Sam Jones. Santa Monica, CA: Fusion Films, 2003. This documentary follows the band Wilco as it records its fourth album, *Yankee Hotel Foxtrot.* It captures the band's difficulty in retaining artistic integrity while dealing with a major record label.

Kurt and Courtney. Directed by Nick Broomfield. Bristol, RI: Wellspring, 1998. This documentary chronicles the life of Kurt Cobain, the lead singer of Nirvana who committed suicide in 1994. The film explores Cobain's struggles with drugs, his relationship with Courtney Love, and some of the conspiracy theories surrounding his death.

The Tomorrow Show with Tom Snyder: Punk and New Wave. Los Angeles: Shout! Factory, 2005. A collection of clips from Tom Snyder's late-night television talk show in the 1970s and 1980s, featuring performances and interviews with the Ramones, Joan Jett, Iggy Pop, John Lyndon, Elvis Costello, Patti Smith, and the Plasmatics.

Web Sites

Epitonic (www.epitonic.com). One of the many Internet sites that includes a section devoted to indie rock. The site provides listener recommendations as well a newsletter and a blog from the editor. It provides links to band biographies and lists of MP3s for hundreds of indie rock bands.

The Future of Music Coalition (www.futureofmusic.org). A nonprofit organization devoted to creating a dialogue between various members of the music community. The organization aims to educate the public, the media, and policy makers about the technological issues affecting musicians and artists.

GarageBand (www.garageband.com). Since 1999 GarageBand has introduced listeners to emerging independent artists and musicians. The site selects and ranks songs, many of which are picked up by one of its one thousand radio partners. The site's aim is to change how music is discovered and promoted.

IndieHQ (www.indiehq.com). IndieHQ provides a forum for indie bands, record labels, and fans of independent music. The site features Indie Nation Podcast, a podcast that highlights indie music, provides interviews with leading indie music leaders and bands, and includes articles about the future of the indie music industry. There is also ample discussion of the latest technological innovation regarding music.

Last FM (www.last.fm/tag). This site provides a list of the most popular indie rock artists, albums, and tracks. It also includes free downloads of indie rock songs.

• Index •

• Picture Credits •

Cover: © Tim Mosenfelder/Getty Images

AP Photo/HO/Courtesy of Sony Pictures Classics/Edward Colver, 36

© Bettmann/Corbis, 17, 26, 28

© Billy Name/Time & Life Pictures/Getty Images, 18

© Bozi/Corbis, 53

© Corbis, 33

© Denis O'Regan/Corbis, 23

© Donald Weber/Getty Images, 69

© Erich Schlegel/Dallas Morning News/Corbis, 52

© Gary A. Livingston/Getty Images, 85

© Getty Images, 67

© Hulton Archive/Getty Images, 20, 32

© John Atashian/Corbis, 57

© Justin Renney/Getty Images, 58-59

© Kevin Scanlon/Getty Images, 83

© Kirk Weddle/Corbis, 55

© Liam Nicholls/Getty Images, 41

© Mike Laye/Corbis, 35

Photos.com, 72, 79

© Randi Lynn Beach/Getty Images, 46

© Reuters/Corbis, 37

© S.I.N./Corbis, 51, 56

© Scott Wintrow/Getty Images, 74

© Steve Pyke/Hulton Archive/Getty Images, 44

© Tim Mosenfelder/Corbis, 9, 82

© Tim Mosenfelder/Getty Images, 10, 42, 73, 77

UrbanImage.tv/Adrian Boot, 21, 30

© Vaugh Youtz/YUMA/Corbis, 13, 63

Jennifer Skancke lives in the vibrant, indie rock rich city of San Francisco, CA. This is her first book for Lucent.